SPAIN, THE CHURCH AND THE ORDERS

SPAIN, THE CHURCH AND THE ORDERS

By

E. ALLISON PEERS

AUTHOR OF "THE SPANISH TRAGEDY"

1939
EYRE AND SPOTTISWOODE
LONDON

First printed - *1939*

PRINTED IN GREAT BRITAIN FOR
EYRE AND SPOTTISWOODE (PUBLISHERS) LIMITED

PREFACE

THIS BOOK is one which I have often thought of writing but have again and again relegated to some other occasion. As a convinced and loyal Anglican who for twenty years has spent one-quarter of his time in the Peninsula, and whose work on Spanish religious history has brought him into exceptionally close contact with certain religious Orders, I have hoped that there might be some interest in my setting down a few little-known facts and personal impressions about the Church and the Orders in Spain. The book I had had in mind would have been a great deal larger than this, and I still hope that in the future the publication of a fuller study will become practicable. But I am compelled to write something now by the mass of ill-informed statements which are being made about the Church in Spain by persons with little or no first-hand knowledge of the subject and the sometimes equally wild statements made in the Church's defence. Whether or no I have been able to give a truer picture than has yet been drawn in this country, I have at least based no arguments on mere hearsay and kept as closely as possible to historical facts and the results of personal observation.

Though it has been impossible to avoid occasional criticism of the writings of others, I have tried to refrain from all unnecessary controversy. It would have been easy to hold up to ridicule criticisms of the Church made in ignorance by persons in high positions whose opinions are too readily credited, but it would not have made for charity. I have preferred to give the true facts and say as little about the critics as possible: they are best forgotten. At the same time, lest I should be thought to be sheltering my friends, I must say with all possible emphasis that I deplore the way in which certain ecclesiastics in the Church of England have written and spoken of the Roman Catholic Church in Spain. One of them went so far as to declare that that Church had "failed, and failed lamentably, to present Christianity faithfully to the nation." Various others made statements which to anyone familiar with Spain at once reveal their ignorance of it. Hardly any of them have expressed sympathy with the Church in Spain in the martyrdom which events not of her own seeking have thrust upon her or with those millions of Spanish Catholics who for so long have been cut off from Christian fellowship and public worship.

And yet it is barely more than a century since the riots which followed the rejection of the second Reform Bill, in 1831, gave Anglican Bishops some faint idea of the meaning of the word persecution.[1] "For months"—till some time after the Reform Bill had become the law of the land—"it was not safe for a bishop to appear in public in any article of sacerdotal dress." "The Archbishop of Canterbury was mobbed in his own cathedral city. . . . The Bishop of Bristol had to escape disguised as a footman. His palace was burned to the ground, and his cathedral only saved by the courage of an aged verger in turning a fire-hose on the infuriated mob."[2] One might have expected that Bishops and Deans whose predecessors had undergone these minor discomforts would realize the magnitude of what the Church in Spain has suffered, and, whatever their political views, would dissociate themselves at least from support of those who must be held responsible for such persecution. Well may Anglicans feel ashamed of leaders who have brought their communion into such notoriety. Well may the Church in Spain feel that she has been wounded in the house of those who should have been her friends.

---

[1] Cf. Philip Usher in *Church Quarterly Review*, April–June 1937, p. 122.
[2] *Ibid.*

By contrast, it is pleasant to refer to an incident which occurred in Spain during the Second Republic and is described by a Protestant commentator. In October 1932, an attack, "apparently the work of Communists," was made upon the Protestant church of Marín, in Galicia, which has the largest Evangelical congregation in the country. "Roman Catholics," records the commentator, "showed a great solidarity of sympathy and flew to our assistance."[1] Is not this small-scale affray a foreshadowing of the world-wide conflict which is surely coming between the organized forces of irreligion and the Church of Christ? When it comes, if the Church is to be victorious, a United Christian Front will be a stern necessity. Can we not prepare the way for that now?

It is as a contribution to the better understanding of a Church which will always be in the vanguard of the struggle against anti-Christ that I offer these few notes on the Church in Spain and on the religious Orders who represent its finest and most enduring virtues.

E. A. P.

December 15, 1938

Note: I am indebted to the Editors of the *Church Times*, *Guardian*, *Tablet*, *Universe* and *Catholic Times* for permission to reproduce material which has appeared in their columns, and also to Messrs. Burns, Oates and Washbourne, who have kindly allowed me to incorporate the substance of a pamphlet entitled *The Church in Spain, 1737–1937*. The full titles of works referred to in the footnotes will be found in the Bibliography.

[1] Araujo and Grubb, *op. cit.*, p. 46.

CONTENTS

CHAPTER I

THE CHURCH IN SPAIN

IT IS of little use to attempt to understand the religious Orders in Spain without knowing something of the characteristics and the position in that country of the Church to which they all render allegiance. Some of this necessary knowledge may be gained from books, though the acrimony with which the Church's enemies attack her and the unwillingness of her defenders (at least in print) to admit the slightest justification for their contentions make this a difficult way of reaching the truth. It is more satisfactory to have lived or travelled in Spain and gleaned first-hand knowledge. This, however, is also apt to be one-sided and incomplete. One-sided, because the observer with definite ideas or convictions cannot fail to view his subject through spectacles of the particular tint which he favours—and too often, strange to say, if he puts questions with the expectation of a particular answer his obliging informant will give him the answer which he is seeking. Incomplete, because the subject is vast, intricate and many-sided, and only after years devoted to the study of it could one hope to treat it at all fully.

This chapter makes no claim to give more than a personal impression, based partly on reading but principally on long familiarity with Spain and the Spanish people. As an Anglican, I have been accustomed to regard the Church in Spain from a critical standpoint; and as a trained investigator I have learned to distinguish between the essential and the non-essential, weigh and sift evidence which the tourist might unquestionably accept and check personal impressions by such oral or written testimony as is available.

I

If the critical reader thinks some of my conclusions over-cautious or unilluminating, he must turn to the bolder assertions of persons who, knowing little or no Spanish, spent a few days in Spain during the Civil War and returned, as perhaps they went, with their minds entirely made up about the Church and her iniquities. For myself, the more I learn, the less inclined I am to draw other than tentative conclusions. But these have at least been formed, not by random conversations in *lingua franca* with a few Spaniards in one or two cities, but from intimate acquaintanceships extending over many years, from the daily companionship of Spanish colleagues in England, from innumerable conversations with complete strangers and from long or short periods spent in Spanish universities, in the families both of Catholics and of free-thinkers, in monasteries and seminaries, in the Residencia de Estudiantes of the Junta para Amplia-ción de Estudios—in places of many kinds representing every phase and aspect of Spanish life.

But perhaps I have found most of the courage to attempt this introductory chapter—for it is not an easy one to write—in the experience of worshipping Sunday by Sunday with my fellow-Christians in Spanish churches. Realizing, at an early stage of my acquaintance with Spain, that my work would continually take me to places where there were no Anglican chaplaincies, I resolved to learn to worship as the Spaniards did, rather than be cut off, for several months in each year, from the means of grace. It has not always been plain sailing and I should subscribe to the Nineteenth Article of Religion with more conviction now than twenty years ago. Not infrequently I have found formalism, materialism and even superstition[1] where I hungered for the pure Word of God. Empty pulpit eloquence, dirty and

---

[1] It was a learned Jesuit, P. Masdeu, who said of his fellow-countrymen in the late eighteenth century: "They are the staunchest defenders of the Faith . . . devout men who, if they go to extremes, incline towards super-stition, not towards impiety." (*Historia crítica de España y de la cultura española*, I, 261-2.) The generalization still holds.

2

ill-kept churches, slovenly behaviour in choir have often proved irritating and distracting. But there have been many compensations, all of which do not exist in Anglican churches at home.

Worshipping, as well as living, with Spaniards has enabled me to view their Church and its problems both sympathetically and critically—from their point of view as well as from my own. And it is from this double standpoint that these pages are written. Here or there I may have been over-exacting; here or there, over-idealistic. But at least I have made an honest attempt to understand both the Church and her critics. And I offer the result, in this its present inadequate form, to all Christian people who will lay aside prejudice and set themselves the ideal of learning and speaking the truth in love, that together we may grow up into Him in all things, which is the head, even Christ.

The first in order of the conclusions which one draws about the Catholic Church in Spain is that it is the Church of the Spanish people.[1] Whether or no we can accept its dogmas and join in its services, acquaintance with the country will at once lead us to that conclusion. It is confirmed by the universally acknowledged fact that no other religious body can describe itself as the Church's serious rival. With the rarest exceptions, individuals who have left it, instead of transferring their allegiance elsewhere, have cut themselves off from institutional Christianity altogether. "The whole nation," wrote Richard Ford in his *Handbook to Spain* (1845), "is divided into two classes—bigoted Romanists or Infidels; there is no *via media*." Not as a result of logical reasoning, but from temperament and according to century-old tradition, the attitude of the Spaniard to the Church is "all or none." In religion, as in politics, he sees

[1] Even Mr. Henry Brinton believes "that the Spanish people are naturally religious and that Roman Catholicism is the form of religion best suited to the people." (*Christianity and Spain*, p. 41.)

3

everything as either black or white; the pendulum swings relentlessly; and the man who can no longer accept Catholic dogma makes no attempt to find a religion less exacting and less unyielding, but goes straight to the other extreme, and either becomes fanatically opposed to all forms of religion (whence perhaps the success of the Anarchist movement and whence undoubtedly the anti-Christian outrages to be chronicled hereafter) or cherishes within his own breast a strictly individual form of personal religion—how far satisfying to him none but he can tell.

Protestantism has found only the slightest degree of acceptance among the Spanish people, and even this has been induced largely by foreign missions. There seems to be in the Spaniard an instinctive aversion from it. "I belong," said the politician Emilio Castelar in 1869, "not to the world of theology and faith but to that of philosophy and reason. But if I were ever to return to the world I have left, I would certainly not embrace the Protestant religion, which freezes my soul, and has been the constant enemy of my country and my race; much rather would I throw myself on my knees again before the . . . altar which has inspired the great sentiments of my life."[1]

To most people unacquainted with Spain that remark would have little meaning; to most foreign Protestants it would be completely incomprehensible. But it might be taken as the starting-point of a detailed study of the Spanish character and it goes far towards explaining the indifferent success of the Protestant Evangelical bodies in Spain, of which their own statistics[2] leave no doubt. In 1933, out of the twenty-three and a half million inhabitants of Spain, the total Evangelical community numbered 21,900 persons, of whom only 6,259 were communicants. These were divided among twenty-five societies, which included missions

[1] M. Menéndez y Pelayo, *Historia de los Heterodoxos Españoles*, VII, 433.
[2] The information in this paragraph is taken from Araujo and Grubb, *op. cit.*

4

organized by English, (Northern) Irish, French, German, Dutch, Swedish and American bodies. Of the 265 workers in the 166 local churches, only 142 were Spaniards.[1] It is fairly clear, then, that Protestantism in Spain is an exotic plant which finds little that is congenial in Spanish soil.

The new facilities given to Protestants and the disabilities of which they were relieved by the Second Republic would be expected to have led to a marked growth had this form of religion any deep roots among the people. That they did not may be gathered from a Protestant Evangelical report written two years after the establishment of the Republic, of which the relevant points (favourable and unfavourable) may here be summarized:

> It seems questionable, therefore, whether there has been any marked expansion of Protestantism in the last thirty or forty years. . . . During (the years 1910–30) there has hardly been noted any progress in evangelical work in Spain. . . . It (*i.e.*, the Protestant community) has tended to become a society for mutual culture rather than a crusade for the spiritual conquest of the nation. . . . The exoticism of much of the work has also been a hindrance. . . . Ministers are almost invariably paid by foreign committees. . . .
>
> A brief review of local conditions will not be out of place here. Galicia is almost exclusively a field of the Brethren, and their work . . . has met with much success. The conditions in the rest of the north of Spain are disappointing. . . . There are three very weak congregations in the province of Huesca. In addition, both here and in the adjacent region of Catalonia, there are ten exceedingly small local groups with very little organization. . . . León is very weakly occupied. The situation on the Mediterranean coast is somewhat more encouraging. . . . Andalusia deserves special mention. Much of the work here . . . has been very disappointing.[2]

[1] *Op. cit.*, pp. 92–4.   [2] *Op. cit.*, pp. 83–90, *passim.*

This seems to need no commentary. It reveals the Spanish Protestants as a number of pathetic little groups of Christians, deeply permeated by foreign influences, making little headway and as seldom turning Catholics from the practice of the religion of their fathers as converting infidels from their denial of it. Though I am bound in candour to record this impression, I should like to add that I have no sort of animus against Spanish Protestants. On the contrary, I honour them for their continuous steadfastness in the most depressing circumstances; my relations with them have been uniformly smooth and cordial; and they have always seemed to me very markedly to commend their religion by their life.

Nevertheless, to pass from Protestantism to Catholicism in Spain is to pass into an atmosphere of intense vitality, and also into an atmosphere which is pre-eminently one of worship, reverence and devotion. Nowhere is the old saying better exemplified that while Protestantism brings a man to his feet Catholicism sends him to his knees. The Catholic Church in Spain is above all a worshipping Church: so much must be clear to any observer—Catholic, Protestant, Moslem, Jew, Agnostic or Atheist. "The fervour of Spanish Catholics," wrote the Madrid correspondent of *The Times* in 1931, "can be tested by simply entering any church any day in the week during Mass hours. On Sundays and feasts the churches are always crowded to their fullest capacity."[1] To anyone who knows Spain that is simply a commonplace which needs no illustration. But for the sake of others let me set down some personal impressions. There is a church in the centre of Madrid which I have visited and attended for many years, on Sundays and week-days, at all hours, according to circumstances. At six o'clock on a Sunday morning, it is crowded—mainly with people of the poorer classes: waiters and chambermaids, small shopkeepers, busy

[1] *The Times*, October 9, 1931.

housewives and the like—and there are as many people leaving the last service as are entering for the next. At seven and eight, it is still full: often there is not a chair to be had and hardly so much as kneeling-room. Young people predominate and there is a considerable sprinkling of men. By nine, the large majority of another packed congregation is formed by men. At ten, for the sung Mass, the worshippers are coming in families, rather than singly. By eleven, though the church is still well filled, one has an impression of the *messe des paresseux*. There are several still later services, which I have never attended. But in that one church, holding perhaps three or four hundred, several thousands must worship every Sunday.

Some English people, especially non-Catholics, will suppose that these congregations are attracted by the magnificence of the ceremonial for which the Roman Church is everywhere famous. On the contrary, it is the Low Masses, without music, incense or even audible words, that attract the greatest crowds: more elaborate services are often comparatively poorly attended. I wish those to whom this comes as a surprise could enter almost any church in a small town or village in the early hours of a day of obligation and see the worshippers kneeling on the cold stone floor, in the most uncomfortable positions, their eyes fixed on the altar, their lips moving as they repeat their familiar childhood prayers, oblivious of everything save their devotions.[1] The two things that chiefly strike one are

[1] Only people thus trained in intense and concentrated habits of devotion could have behaved as they did at a memorable Mass (December 22, 1937) in besieged Teruel with the enemy's batteries a hundred yards distant. As the officiating Dominican Father was about to administer Communion to the congregation, a shell burst outside the church—the first of that day. "I was already turned towards the people," he records, "and I said a few words to them of encouragement and cheer. . . . The Lord must have spoken through me, for they all remained quiet and the Communion proceeded without further incident." The whole of the moving narrative of the religious observances and spiritual experiences of the besieged Nationalists in Teruel, by P. Emilio Saura, O.P., from which this episode is taken, merits publication in English. It will be found in a privately circulated publication, *De Rebus Hispaniae*, Burgos, June 30, 1938, fols. 19–22.

the darkness—for Spanish churches seldom have large east windows—and the silence. It is perhaps the silence that makes the most striking impression on the stranger—an indelible impression of startling contrast. So volatile and vivacious, so good a talker, is the Spaniard in his daily life; so still, so tranquil and so recollected—so good a listener— as he communes with his God.

Catholicism, with its emphasis on individual devotion and the reverent attitude of worship, provides the atmosphere in which a people of the peculiarly individualistic and mystical Spanish temperament can best develop its spiritual life; and it is only fair that we should here insist upon the excellences of distinctively Spanish Catholicism because later we shall have to consider some of its defects. One of the reasons for the slightness of the appeal made to Spaniards by Protestantism is probably that their temperament is in all essentials so profoundly and realistically mystical. It is not for nothing that in Spain, as nowhere else since the Renaissance, mysticism has flourished. As you walk through a great cathedral, in which not nuns but women with market-baskets by their side are kneeling at their prayers, so absorbed that you can almost touch them without their being aware of your presence;[1] as you pass and re-pass a man—not a monk, but a shabbily dressed, middle-aged labourer—contemplating the figure of Christ crucified, and ere he leaves it, see him edge forward and kiss the tip of His feet, you begin to realize that this is a country which knows true religion, personal religion, the religion of God and the soul—a country for which, not in vain, St. John of the Cross wrote those maxims so many of which often seem to us so impossible of fulfilment:

[1] Cf. the testimony of Havelock Ellis: "We realize how far we are from the present when we enter a Spanish church. The ecstatic attitude of devotion which the worshippers sometimes fall into without thought of any observer is equally unlike the elegant grace of the French worshipper or the rigid decorum of the English." (*The Soul of Spain*, p. 13.)

Feed not thy spirit on aught beside God. . . .

Find spiritual tranquillity in a loving attentiveness to
God. . . .

Let Christ crucified be sufficient for thee. . . .

The soul that walks in love wearies not neither is
wearied. . . .

Wisdom enters through love, silence and mortification . . .

Keep silence and have continual converse with
God. . . .

Walk in solitude with God. . . .

Live in this world as though there were in it but God
and thy soul, so that thy heart may be detained
by naught that is human.[1]

Has the reader ever attended a High Mass in France? If
so, he will recall the atmosphere of unrest, the bangings and
chatterings, the obtrusive entrances of late-comers, the old
ladies collecting the eternal halfpence and giving noisy
change, the continual clinking of coins which ceases only
for a few moments during the Consecration, the irate matron
who discovers that her own private chair has been appropriated and almost pulls it from under the unconscious
offender—all this and a great deal more which my pen lacks
the cunning to describe. Let him contrast this with the
quiet recollectedness of a Spanish High Mass—the contrast
is as striking as between the behaviour of the railway porters
at Hendaye and at Irún: the former rush at you with shouts
and gesticulations; the latter stand silently gazing at you or
pad noiselessly along in your wake.

I can understand the feelings of a devout Anglican or
Nonconformist who is bewildered by all in a Spanish church
that is quite incomprehensible to him and who misses and
longs for the familiar hymns, lessons, prayers and sermons
in his own language and the homely atmosphere of the

[1] *Complete Works of St. John of the Cross*, London, 1934–5, III, 250 ff.

church of his baptism, which he left behind him when he set out for Spain. I can understand the position of a foreign tourist who finds so much of interest in the country that for one reason or another he never enters churches during service hours or observes the congregations and so never considers this matter at all. But I cannot understand any English Christian who sees in Spain what I have described and does not yearn for a like assiduity in worship and a like devoutness at home.

What would the vicar of an Anglican parish think if, just for one Sunday, his church were invaded, at eleven o'clock Mattins, by as many people as attend a church in a Spanish parish of similar size on every Sunday, not to speak of many week-days, throughout the year? If his comfortable pews had to be taken away and the church left half-empty of furniture to make room for the crowds, who came, not to listen to elaborate anthems or sermons with attractive titles, still less because it was the hall-mark of respectability to attend church once on Sunday, but *to pray*? Surely, he would say, some great revival of religion has begun—and he would be right. Yet this *is* what happens in Spain; and there is a reason for it. Your hostile critic puts forward one unworthy reason after another and is generally satisfied that some one—or possibly every one—of them is correct. But if he will live in Spain and become intimate with Spanish life he will find that each of these reasons breaks down. Custom, convention, apprehensiveness of the future, desire to be thought well of and a dozen other causes may no doubt be responsible for a small minority of church-goers in Spain, as everywhere. But such causes can never account for more than a small minority and they leave entirely untouched the spirit of devotion which at all times permeates the country. There is only one thing that will account for that—*the love of God*.

"The religious fervour in the churches here," remarked an experienced newspaper correspondent behind the Nationalist lines in 1937, "is one of the most extraordinary

sights I have ever witnessed in my life. I never thought I
would live to see private soldiers get up voluntarily at six
o'clock in the morning to attend Mass. You would have to
wait a long time before you saw Tommy Atkins do that.
. . . I often saw English R.C. Tommies go to confession
in little, battered churches at the Front during the Great
War, but they went behind a curtain at the side of the
confessional, whereas here only women go behind the
curtain: men kneel down by the half-door at the entrance
to the box, in sight of all the people. I have seen captains,
majors, colonels and even generals kneel humbly there,
after waiting their turn among private soldiers and N.C.O.s,
and it made me think hard. A man who humbles himself
like that must believe."[1]

The life of the community—especially in the village and
small town—centres in the Church and the Church's year
to a degree that few would credit. The holiday is still the
holy day and the holy day the holiday. The village revel
begins, as it were, soon after dawn, with Mass in the village
church.[2] The pilgrimage, as in mediaeval times, is still an
occasion for simple and happy fellowship.[3] Many centuries
have passed since, throughout Western Europe, drama
emerged from the church into the city; in Spain, as one
watches the crowded street processions of Semana Santa, so
closely intertwined with the life of the people, one feels that
it might have so emerged but yesterday.

It is true that, by comparison with the inconceivably high
standards of past generations, religious observance in Spain
is not what it was. One recent writer has even spoken of
"the progressive and lamentable decadence of the religious

[1] Sir Percival Phillips, as reported by Francis McCullagh: *In Franco's
Spain*, pp. 129–30.
[2] Cf. p. 184, below.
[3] In a short essay there is no space to enlarge upon this, as I could, from
experience, but those who are interested will find the atmosphere of the
pilgrimage and the *fiesta* remarkably well reproduced in Professor Walter
Starkie's brilliant picture, *Spanish Raggle-Taggle* (London, 1934), notably in
Chapters XI to XIII.

convictions of the nation."[1] Invasions of the country by the towns; migrations to the towns from the country; rises in the cost of living coupled with the miserable incomes both of laity and of clergy; the growing influence of freemasonry; the effectiveness of Communist and Anarchist propaganda —all these and other causes have led in places to a partial deca olicizing of sections of the population.[2] But much ground has been recovered through Catholic Action—the first National Congress of which was held in Spain as recently as November 1929. In this religious and non-   ty movement, "the true Crusade of modern times,"[3] the laity co-operate with the clergy, penetrating where the clergy cannot, in order to intensify the hold of religion on the people. If we take the country as a whole, religion is still the Spaniard's principal reality. One hardly ever seems to find people, even in the poorest classes, as one does in England, whom religious influences have completely failed to touch—who cannot remember having so much as entered a place of worship, who are ignorant of what the Church stands for, to whom the central facts of religion are without meaning. That fact speaks volumes.

Travellers often bring back tales of the "easy familiarity" of Spaniards with their Church. It is not perhaps an unmixed virtue. It has its defects, one of which is that carelessness and even slovenliness of choristers and servers which often shocks foreigners. But none the less it is at its best a most attractive thing. During the early months of the Civil War a mother was taking refuge in a partially demolished church with her small children, who were playing about among the wreckage. Seeing a priest approaching, she hurriedly reproved them. Not so the priest.

[1] Mendizábal, *op. cit.*, p. 147.
[2] P. Francisco Peiró, in his sincere and moving little book, *El Problema religioso-social de España*, gives some depressing statistics of the shortage of clergy in certain parts of Spain and the depleted church attendances. But he is dealing with specific cases, not with general impressions.
[3] Gomá, *op. cit.*, I, 285.

"Why are you stopping them?" he asked. "Let them go on playing."

"But this is still a church . . . ?" she replied.

"Yes," rejoined the priest, "*that's just the point.*"[1]

Only in a country of Catholic tradition—perhaps only in Spain—would that point have been clear without implification. Spanish Catholics are *bien amistados con Dios.*[2] A church is no gloomy place, but the house of our Father. When we enter it, we try to leave sinful thoughts outside but not happy thoughts. We feel at home in it and we see no irreverence in treating it as our home. The classical illustration usually given of this is the ritual Dance of the Seises in the great Cathedral of Seville—the consecration to God of the most instinctive pleasure of the Spanish people —which also illustrates one of the traits of Spanish Catholicism which northerners find it so difficult to understand: the closeness of the connection in Spain between religion and art.[3] That Dance has been described too often for a fresh description to be either necessary or desirable.[4] I would rather refer to an unrehearsed dance that I once saw in the same Cathedral, which is so large and has so many

---

[1] Pemán, *op. cit.*, p. 111.

[2] Cf. Havelock Ellis (*op. cit.*, p. 14): "It would be a serious mistake to see here any indifference to religion; on the contrary, this easy familiarity with sacred things is simply the attitude of those who, in Wordsworth's phrase, 'lie in Abraham's bosom all the year,' and do not, as often among ourselves, enter a church once a week to prove how severely respectable, for the example of others, they can on occasion show themselves to be. It was thus that our own ancestors, whose faith was assuredly less questioning than ours, made themselves at home in the aisles of Old St. Paul's."

[3] On this matter, and also on the Spaniard's religious sense in general, some illuminating remarks have been made by Ángel Ganivet, in his *Idearium Español* (see especially pp. 5, 28, 76, in the second edition, Madrid, 1905). Ganivet was by no means an orthodox Catholic but he understood the character of his compatriots as few others have done. Particularly interesting are his reflections on the passionate attachment of Spain to the dogma of the Immaculate Conception. "Surely," he surmises, "there must be some mystery beneath this dogma which by hidden ways links itself with our national soul."

[4] Notably by E. M. Whishaw in *My Spanish Year*, London, 1914, pp. 150–73, and by J. B. Trend, in *Spain from the South*, London, 1928, pp. 54–61. Havelock Ellis also has an essay on Spanish dancing (*op. cit.*, pp. 170–90).

doors that it is often used as a short cut across the city. Two little mites, of perhaps five years of age, came tripping in at the south-west door, paused each to cover her head with an absurd little square of handkerchief and to make a reverence to the Altar, and then went tripping across the nave to the north-east door as naturally as two lambs gam-bolling in the sunshine.

Contrast with this another scene I have witnessed. A fine summer evening in a glass-enclosed hotel restaurant on the promenade of a famous Spanish seaside resort. A fashionable crowd of diners—mostly Madrid folk come up to the north coast to escape the heat. Loud and animated conversation—and anyone who has dined in Spanish restaurants knows how loud that can be. Suddenly the tinkle of a bell in the street outside—and through the window one sees a vested priest across the way carrying the Sacrament to some dying person. Instantly the talking ceases. Half the diners and the whole of the waiters go down on their knees. To some of the foreigners present, who make an awkward and uneasy attempt at half-rising, the thing is inexplicable. To the Spaniard, on the other hand, it is perfectly natural. He sees, not a boy and a bell and a priest, but God. The King of Glory. . . . The superficialities of life have suddenly been invaded by a swift solemnity which in Protestant countries is unknown save when some such function as a banquet is visited by death. . . . The little procession is gone and in a minute or two one is imagining the interlude to have been a dream; but the tribute paid to Eternal Reality has been a tribute also to the reality of religion to the Spanish people.

What, then, must the fervour and emotion of the Spaniard have been in those great moments of religious exaltation which came to the country during the Civil War. Many of them have already been described; others still await their chronicler. The clandestine Masses said in innumerable private houses in Republican Spain by priests in overalls disguised as "workers" or militiamen. The little companies of the faithful, meeting on the Maundy Thursday and Good Friday of 1937, to keep vigil in spirit before an invisible Altar of Repose in the Spain that had no Easter. No tangible *monumento* for them to visit; no Real Presence, in the theological sense, for them to adore; but the unfailing Real Presence promised by Christ to the two or three gathered together in His Name and the blessing assured to those persecuted ones who hunger and thirst after God.[1]

In "redeemed" Spain—*España blanca,* as Catholics have loved to call it—the emotions engendered could be given free expression. Some of the deepest feelings, in every town and village conquered, must have been aroused by the sight of the churches profaned, dismantled and perhaps partially burned, though not as a rule completely destroyed. Furniture broken up for firewood; piles of broken statuary swept aside into some corner; kitchen utensils strewn everywhere, with remains of hurried meals; here and there, perhaps, an ammunition dump or a disused motor-car. But, amid all this destruction and sacrilege, one sign of the victory of religion over impiety has already been restored: a little oil sanctuary-lamp is burning and on the Altar are two lighted candles. "As though in haste, as though with impatience, asking for no more luxurious home, God has returned to His temple. Behold Him here speaking words of Divine love even before an end has been made of the signs of human hatred."[2]

And what of the more spectacular scenes? Who can measure, or conceive, the depth of feeling behind those Midnight Masses of Christmas, said on the snow-covered battlefield, sometimes high in the mountains, with the snow

---

[1] E. Allison Peers: "The Spain that has no Easter," in *The Tablet,* March 27, 1937.
[2] Pemán, *op. cit.,* p. 110.

cleared from a slab of rock to make an altar,[1] and a congregation of soldiers, who had come from setting up their rudely fashioned *nacimientos* in the trenches as though they had been at home. Who can estimate the intensity of the spiritual life of those young soldiers of the Juventud Católica with their rule of daily Mass, even in the trenches, and evening prayers said together, with a closing petition for their enemies?[2] "One Army chaplain," reports a visitor to the Nationalist front, "told me that in the beleaguered University City in Madrid they had had all the Holy Week services in full, and on most fronts the Altar of Repose was set up in a dug-out and guarded fervently day and night."[3]

Or who can imagine that first Mass said on the reconquered Hill of the Angels, beneath the grandiose dome of a blue Castilian sky, so near the battlefield that the voices of the choir were at times drowned by the noise of the cannon? The monument set up some years since by Spanish devotion had been shot to pieces but the stone Heart had been roughly pieced together and around it loving hands had placed heaps of red roses. An altar had been improvised: nothing more.

And in presence of that ruin—one might say, humanly speaking, of that catastrophe—of splintered stone, in the freshness of the early morning, a choir made up of

[1] See Bayle, *op. cit.*, *passim*, and in particular the photograph (p. 31) of the Epiphany Mass in the snows of the Alto de la Cabra (6,300 feet), January 6, 1937.

[2] Alfonso de Zulueta: "Impressions of National Spain," in *The Tablet*, June 18, 1938. The text of the nightly petition, as given by this writer, is as follows:

"O Lord, Who commandest us to love our enemies, and Who desirest not the death of the sinner, but that he should be converted and live: hear our prayer and grant the grace of final repentance to those who die fighting against Thee on the battlefields. May Divine Mercy shine by the side of human justice, so that our enemies may not be so unfortunate as to lose Eternal Life together with their earthly existence. We unite our petition with that which Jesus Christ offered Thee from the Cross, when, looking on His executioners, He asked forgiveness for them. We beg it of Thee, O God of battles, Who livest and reignest for ever and ever. Amen."

[3] *Ibid.*

requetés from Navarre, with their unspoiled peasant voices, intoned those eternal, unchanging words:
Credo in unum Deum, Patrem Omnipotentem. . . .

When one knows something of the Spaniard's everyday religion one can well understand to what white heat the attacks on it by its enemies have moved him and with what deep thanksgiving he finds himself free, in White Spain, to follow it once more without hindrance.

Since one of the aims of this book is to examine certain criticisms which have been levelled against the Church in Spain, no apology will be necessary for entering upon them thus early. Some of them will be found to be justified; others will not. Presumably no Church is perfect. Quite a number of these criticisms come from Catholics—and by no means always those criticisms with the most truth in them. English Catholics do not always realize that Catholics and Catholic practice vary a great deal according to national temperament; and some of them, I think, perhaps with a laudable desire not to be prejudiced in favour of their co-religionists, have accepted, repeated or proferred criticisms of them without being really qualified to express an opinion.

A recent statement by Mr. Anthony Crossley, M.P., describes the Church in Spain as being "far from what I would regard as a model for the principles which the Catholic Church ought to hold and display. Its cardinal sin is that it was rich in a land of poverty."[1] That will be a convenient starting-point for our examination, since the charge of enjoying excessive wealth has been levelled against the Church in Spain for centuries—ever since the days, in fact, when it was true!

It is, of course, a matter of history that there was a time

[1] *The Tablet*, January 9, 1937 ("A Visit to Nationalist Spain"). Cf. leading article of January 30, 1937: "The Church in Spain had many imperfections, etc."

17

when the Church was over-endowed and under-taxed, but
that was centuries ago. In mid-sixteenth century the total
income drawn from its real estate was no less than five
million ducats, or half the income of the entire kingdom,
and one-fifth of this sum belonged to the forty-six archbishops and bishops.[1] This was indeed wealth. Against
this fact may be set others—e.g., that the Crown drew
frequently upon it and also that much of it went to feed the
poor, and to provide schools, hospitals, asylums, and other
institutions many of which to-day, in our own country, are
provided by municipalities or by the State. At the beginning of the nineteenth century neither the wealth of the
Church nor the calls made on it had greatly diminished.
The Archbishop of Toledo enjoyed an annual income of
£120,000; the Archbishop of Valencia, £32,000; the Bishop
of Murcia, £21,000. Canonries and other dignities were
remunerated proportionately. The Orders were also
wealthy; the Escorial Monastery, for example, which at
that time belonged to the Hieronymites, had £28,000
annually.[2] But taxes were very heavy. If worth more than
300 ducats (about £33) per annum, every ecclesiastical
benefice or dignity to which the King nominated paid a
tax of six months' income on appointment; if worth less, its
tax was proportionately smaller. Once in every fifteen
years, six months' income was payable on all benefices
attached to corporations in mortmain. The revenue of all
ecclesiastical offices went to the State while they were
vacant, together with the revenues of all suppressed religious
congregations. Every cathedral and collegiate benefice
and all other benefices not conveying the cure of souls and
worth over £66 per annum paid one-third of their revenue to
the King annually. This tax alone is calculated to have
brought in £175,000 a year. There was also a smaller tax

[1] Altamira, op. cit., III, 344.
[2] The amounts given are in round figures and calculated from those of
Laborde (op. cit., V, 17) at the parity rate of 100 reales to the pound sterling.

on less valuable benefices. Then there was a system of "voluntary" gifts, some of which still survive, payable to the State by the clergy to compensate for remission of some, though not all, of the taxes paid by the laity.[1] Finally (omitting several less important taxes) there was the rather overpowering provision that the King might legally dispose of one-third of the income of all the sees—a tax alone, this, of 6s. 8d. in the pound! "This right," however, the contemporary historian assures us, "is exercised with great moderation. Its amount is not drawn out in one gross sum, but pensions and sums destined for objects of public utility are assigned on the revenues of the various sees, but hardly ever amounting to one-fourth of their income."[2]

Besides paying these direct and indirect taxes, the Bishops did a vast amount of charitable work now performed by public benefactors or by the State. Antequera, in his classical work on *desamortización*, tells of a Bishop of Plasencia who in eight months of the years 1801–2 had allotted £15,000 to works of charity, which included the provision of a home for three hundred orphan children. Laborde, the historian previously quoted, gives a more comprehensive picture.

> From the period of the reconquest of Spain from the Moors, most of the public establishments owe their foundation to the clergy, by whom also whole towns have been rebuilt and raised from their ruins. The most beautiful aqueducts, fountains and public walks in the cities have been constructed at the expense of the bishops; from them also the poor have received the most effectual relief in times of scarcity, epidemic disease and war. The Bishop of Orense converted his episcopal palace into an alms-house [for French clerics exiled during the Revolution]. Cardinal Orenzana, Archbishop of Toledo, converted the alcazar of that city . . . into an establishment wherein are received two hundred children and

---

[1] Laborde, *op. cit.*, pp. 30–2.   [2] *Op. cit.*, pp. 32–3.

seven hundred poor persons of all ages. The Bishop of
Cordoba, during the scarcity of 1804, and for a long time
afterwards, made a daily distribution of twelve hundred
rations of bread to the poor inhabitants of his diocese.
The aqueduct which conveys water to the city of Tarragona is the work of their archbishop.[1]

There were innumerable calls, then, both voluntary and
compulsory, upon the wealth of the hierarchy. None the
less, their gross wealth was undoubtedly very large. It is
commonly said by historians that in the middle of the
eighteenth century the Church owned about one-third of
the land in the country. One can quite believe that the
generalization, though unsupported by figures, was at least
approximately true.

But will it be credited that there are still those who repeat
this phrase and apply it to the Church to-day? The Spanish
Bishops, in their letter addressed, in July 1937, "to the
Bishops of the whole world," thought it necessary to treat
seriously a statement that the Church "owned one-third of
the national territory."[2] "It was the biggest landowner in
a country of big landowners," says a recent writer in the
Manchester Guardian.[3] "Its wealth has been estimated at
one-third of the national wealth."[4] These writers would
have been about a century behind the times in the days of
George Borrow—let us say they are about two centuries
behind the times to-day. And they then wonder why people
who know anything about Spanish history are impatient
with them. As a later chapter of this book will show, the
Church was during the early nineteenth century mulcted
of almost the whole of its real estate (which, after all, it came
by quite honestly, and had a perfect right to hold). If it had
become the "biggest landowner" in Spain, it would have

[1] *Op. cit.*, p. 35. [2] *Joint Letter*, p. 25.
[3] *Manchester Guardian*, June 24, 1937. Cf. quotation from *Church Times*,
p. 23 n., 1, below.
[4] Gannes and Repard: *Spain in Revolt*, London, 1936, pp. 225–8.

had to accomplish that feat in the eighty years between the dates of the Concordat and the Second Republic: a task unlikely of achievement when other landowners had had several centuries' start.

The truth is that, at the present time, with occasional exceptions in the shape of property newly acquired, neither regulars nor seculars have any land beyond that on which their buildings stand, fields and gardens, the products of which are used by monks for their own sustenance, and so on. "The Church," declare the Bishops, "possessed no more than a few insignificant pieces of land, presbyteries and buildings devoted to education; and even these last had recently been confiscated by the State. The whole of the possessions of the Church in Spain would not cover a quarter of her needs and she uses them to fulfil the most sacred obligations."[1]

During the Second Republic one sometimes saw statements, circulated for purposes of political propaganda, giving apparently colossal figures as the value of the Church's possessions.[2] Obviously, in a country where most large towns have scores of churches—not to speak of monasteries, convents, seminaries, schools, etc.—and there is a church in every village, however small, the total value of either the buildings or the land on which they stand is going to be very large, especially if the sum is expressed in pesetas— *i.e.*, multiples, at par, of ninepence-halfpenny. It would probably surprise most readers to know that the Protestant Evangelical churches of Spain own property of the total nominal value of 5,519,247 pesetas.[3] If this is true of a small community of 21,900 souls, whose churches, where they have any, are small and insignificant, what must be the nominal value of the property of a Church claiming about one thousand times as many adherents? What huge

---

[1] *Joint Letter*, p. 25.
[2] Cf., for example, Juan Guixé, *op. cit.*, p. 86.
[3] Araujo and Grubb, *op. cit.*, p. 94.

sum would not one think essential for the needs of 20,000 parishes and 30,000 churches? Yet the figures given by Government spokesmen in the Cortes during the debates on the position of the Church showed a total of only 161,000,000 pesetas in real estate, or almost exactly one-sixteenth of the total of three-quarters of a century earlier—that of the year 1857, when disentailment had run a part of its course.

"The story of the Church as the largest landed proprietor in Spain," says Dr. Borkenau—no clerical—"is a myth."[1] Thus, very properly, he deprecates undue credibility. But is he not himself over-credible when he describes the Church as "the largest capitalist" and "the richest shareholder" in the country?[2] This kind of accusation is made continually and without the production of any kind of evidence. In an Appendix are detailed some attempts to track down these statements to their origins, the result of which is that not a shred of authority has been produced for any one of them. The general procedure seems to be that fantastic tales current among the Church's enemies in Spain are published in left-wing newspapers there; are copied by left-wing international organizations and so get into print (losing nothing in the process) in England; are quoted in speeches and letters to newspapers of all shades of opinion (again losing nothing in transit); and are then frequently accepted by unsuspecting readers of these newspapers, who, thinking that whatever appears in their favourite paper must be true, and, not realizing that they are propagandist stories tainted at the source, pass them innocently on. I hope that this book will serve to put well-meaning people on their guard against this type of assertion.

How ludicrous this propaganda is may be judged by the following synthesis of a few of the statements which have appeared in the Press and in books during the last two years.

---

[1] *The Spanish Cockpit*, p. 8.   [2] *Op. cit.*, p. 9.

The Church is (or was) "the greatest landowner in Spain";[1] the "biggest proprietor of land and buildings";[2] "Spain's greatest landlord";[3] in 1931 it "had a direct and indirect control of nearly half the capital of the entire country."[4] It is (or was) "the most important industrialist, banker, schoolmaster and money-lender";[5] it "operated hotels and factories, owned department stores, numerous electric power plants, newspapers, etc.";[6] "owned or controlled . . . the tramway system of Madrid and the Bank of the Holy Ghost (one of the biggest in Spain)";[7] "controlled much slum property in the cities; held a considerable interest in urban transport, in the Underground Railway, 'buses and tramways, etc., both in Barcelona and Madrid. . . . It was the largest individual stockholder in telephones, lumber, contract engineering and electricity. It owned mines in Spain and in Morocco. It held controlling interest in *El Sigla* [*sic*] and *El Aguilar* chain-stores. It had interests in film production, cinemas, theatres, cafés, hotels, sports grounds. It owned dog-racing tracks and bull-rings. Through holding companies it gathered a tithe from the profits of Madrid's most *risqué* cabarets. Other cabarets, including the notorious *Novo Mundo* [*sic*] in Saragossa, it controlled entirely."[8]

The Jesuits "controlled banks, mines and electrical companies, not to mention colleges and newspapers. In Barcelona they owned a large department store."[9] They owned a certain bank in Madrid "with a capital of 126,000,000 pesetas" and "four smaller provincial banks

[1] *Church Times*, January 8, 1937.
[2] E. Conze: *Spain To-day*, London, 1936, p. 25.
[3] Gannes and Repard, *op. cit.*, pp. 225–8.
[4] H. Brinton: *Christianity and Spain*, London, 1938, p. 17.
[5] Gannes and Repard, *op. cit.*, pp. 225–8.
[6] L. Fischer: *Why Spain fights on*, p. 17.
[7] W. B. Gibson in *The Listener*, January 19, 1938. Cf. p. 200, below.
[8] From a propagandist sheet entitled *The War in Spain* (No. 4, February 12, 1938). It is attributed to "a Catholic," whose name is not given.
[9] From a propagandist sheet entitled *Comment* (No. 4, August 7, 1937). It is attributed to "a correspondent who resides in Spain and is an outstanding authority on Spanish history." His name is not given.

with a total capital of 85,000,000 pesetas."[1] They also controlled "about thirty-five business enterprises of big scale, one powerful wireless station, a newsagency, more than sixty newspapers in Madrid and the provinces together with a good many theatres and cinemas."[2]

Any person of sense has only to read this summary (which might be greatly enlarged) to realize that the assertions made about the Church's "wealth" belong to the genus snowball and are likely to contain about as much truth as the child's tale of the immense herd of elephants in the field over the way which proved to be Farmer Brown's peaceful old dun cow.

Not that English propaganda, even at its most ridiculous, can quite approach the best efforts made in Spain. A book written in 1937 by a Spanish Anarcho-Syndicalist,[3] of the type who talks about the "claws" of priests, monks and Jesuits, asserts that in money matters "not a peseta changed hands which was not under the control of the soutane," that "convents, rectories and episcopal residences were financial centres in which were reflected all the fluctuations of Spanish finance" and that the Society of Jesus not only "had the largest holdings in the Spanish railways" but "controlled all the tramways, electricity and gas services, maritime transport services, banks and telephone system." It had (the author tells us on one page) a capital of over *six million* pesetas invested in big business; on another page he calls it *six thousand million*. It probably makes little difference. For it is a matter of history, as we shall see, that in February 1932 the Society of Jesus was dissolved in Spain and its property nationalized.

It would be difficult for any English propagandist to produce anything quite so ridiculous as this last paragraph.

[1] Gannes and Repard, *op. cit.*, pp. 225–8.
[2] Report of an address by W. Horsfall Carter, in *International Affairs*, September–October, 1936, p. 669.
[3] *Proceso histórico de la Revolución Española*, Barcelona, 1937.

Let us take one more example of the nonsense talked about the Church's "wealth"—this time to illustrate the process through which these stories pass. We have seen that historians have said that some two centuries ago the *Church* owned one-third of the *land* of Spain and that certain propagandists have repeated this statement and applied it to the present day. This might be thought bad enough, but what follows is worse. Not content with telling this story about the Church as a whole, they apply it to one specific society within the Church—the Jesuits—and not content with applying it to *land*, they apply it to the *industrial wealth*, and even to the *total wealth*, of the country. Thus:

> The Society of Jesus is said to own one-third of the industrial wealth of the country.[1]
> It was pointed out in the Cortes in 1931 that the Jesuits owned one-third of the total wealth of Spain.[2]

What is the truth? Probably that, as one anti-clerical has put it, with an irony that was presumably unconscious, "there are no statistics on the wealth of the Church; there are only estimates."[3]

A few positive observations, however, need to be made. The first is on the use of the word Jesuit. In Spanish controversy, from which most of our English material directly or indirectly derives, this word has become practically meaningless. In Spain one calls anything of which one strongly disapproves "Jesuitical": "the Jesuit Gil Robles," for example, is an absurd but current phrase, and, on the other side, the members of a well-known Liberal group are often referred to as "the Jesuits of the Left." "*El Socialista*," a left-wing writer tells us, "hints at Jesuitic money in *Claridad*. *Claridad* is eloquent about the Jesuitic perfidy of

---

[1] *Time and Tide*, August 8, 1936.
[2] M. Mitchell, *Storm over Spain*, London, 1937, p. 53.
[3] H. E. Kaminski, *Ceux de Barcelone*, Paris, 1937, p. 194.

El Socialista."[1] When such transference of epithets is possible of two Socialist and anti-clerical newspapers, how much more common is it likely to be in the war of Left against Right! If a right-wing capitalist particularly unpopular with the Left is known to have a large holding in a certain business, it is taking hardly more than a single step to describe the business as "owned by the Jesuits."

Secondly, what is likely to be the truth about the amount of the Church's "wealth"? It will be clear from later chapters that by 1851 repeated acts of spoliation had left the Church as a whole with almost nothing and the Orders with nothing whatever: anything that Church and Orders may possess will have come through gifts and legacies acquired since that date. That the total amount of these may be quite considerable I should think very likely; for the loyalty of Spaniards to their Church is as steadfast as their generosity is proverbial, and there is no need to urge upon them (in the words of a seventeenth-century tombstone inscription which I came upon recently) "whether it be not a sort of Sacrilege to Sweep all away from the Church and Charity into the Possession of their Lay Kindred who are not Needy." But from what I know of religious life in Spain I should expect that by far the largest part of the total amount would go to the Orders, who, as will later be seen, are continually disbursing money in large-scale charitable work, both social and educational, voluntarily accepting responsibilities which ought long since to have been undertaken by the State and saving the State many millions of pounds yearly.

Now it is obvious that any corporation which day after day feeds, clothes and educates the poor without charge must have money to do it with, and as no religious Order would be foolish enough to keep its capital in a stocking, it presumably has invested funds. No doubt this simple

[1] E. Conze, *op. cit.*, p. 61.

fact is the dun cow which the imagination of polemists has transformed into a herd of elephants.) It is equally to be presumed that the Salvation Army and Dr. Barnardo's Homes possess invested funds, but nobody accuses these excellent charitable institutions of controlling chain-stores, or of owning banks, tramway systems and the London Underground Railways. Possibly if the war against God gains ground in England the day will come when they may be so accused. It will then have to be pointed out on their behalf, as I am now pointing out on behalf of the Spanish Orders, that they hold their capital as trustees for the welfare of that section of the community which they voluntarily benefit. And "a trustee is not regarded as rich," as Mr. Arnold Lunn remarks in his brilliant essay in controversy, *Spanish Rehearsal*, "merely because he administers the estate of a millionaire. The Spanish ecclesiastics were the under-paid trustees of national charity."[1]

A third observation concerns the use of wealth. Is there, provided it is honestly acquired and rightly used, any reason why the Church should not handle great wealth? "My own opinion," writes Don Enrique Moreno, a Catholic highly critical of his Church and strongly opposed to the attitude of the hierarchy to the Civil War, "is that wealth has never been an obstacle which hinders the clergy from influencing the masses." He regrets that this argument, "used relent-lessly by every form of propaganda, prevents the considera-tion of other problems."[2] Certainly the wealth of the Church in Spain during the sixteenth and seventeenth centuries was no handicap to her influence.

Were the possessions, great or small, of the Church, or of any one Order, used to keep ministers of the Church in idleness or luxury, they might well be regarded as demora-lizing. Did Spanish religious or clergy live in the state of comfort enjoyed by the Fellows of an Oxford or a Cambridge

[1] *Op. cit.*, p. 234.   [2] *Catholics and the Spanish State*, p. 13.

college, there might be a case for regarding Church wealth as being wasted in riotous living. But, as it is, those who attack the Church on that score would do better to turn their attention to our older Universities. There is nothing for them to do in Spain. Nearly all the money spent there by the Church and the Orders goes in the maintenance of Divine worship—duty to God—or in works of charity—duty to man. Priests, monks, and nuns live in conditions varying between the smallest possible degree of comfort and a point approximating to starvation.[1] Not only have episcopal palaces in Spain few of the solid comforts (which some would call luxuries) of their Anglican counterparts but to a parish priest in Spain the ordinary Anglican vicarage or the snug rooms of a college don would seem plutocratic beyond his dreams.

Let us try to form an opinion of what life is like for the clergy in Spain. Statistics are readily available.[2] We shall begin at the top and work downwards. The Cardinal Archbishop of Toledo, Primate of Spain, receives a stipend of 40,000 pesetas (£1,600) together with an additional 5,000 pesetas (£200) in virtue of his Cardinalate. The Archbishops of Valencia and Seville receive 37,500 each (£1,500); of Santiago and Granada, 32,500 each (£1,300). The Bishops of Barcelona and Madrid receive 27,500 each (£1,100); the remaining Bishops, from 10,000 (£400) to 22,000 (£880) each. To these sums may be added allowances for expenses which vary from 5,000 pesetas (£200) to nothing.

Compare those figures with the stipends of the hierarchy in the Church of England. The Archbishop of Canterbury receives £15,000—nearly nine times as much as the Archbishop of Toledo; the Archbishop of York, £9,000; the Bishop of London, £10,000; the Bishop of Durham, £7,000; the Bishops of Salisbury, Oxford and Bath and Wells, £5,000 each; and, with the exception of three who average

---

[1] Cf. Gomá, *op. cit.*, I, 157–8.
[2] All these figures are taken from Güenechea, *op. cit.*, pp 67–72 *et passim*.

about £2,500, the remaining Bishops receive from £3,000 to £4,500.

The hierarchy of the State Church in England, then, receives from four to nine times the income of the hierarchy of what was the State Church in Spain. One begins to see why the luxury of Lambeth is not to be found in Toledo.

Compare, again, the stipends of the head of the Spanish Church with those of the head of the State. Against the £1,800 of the Spanish Primate, and his £200 for expenses must be set the yearly sum of £40,000 (1,000,000 pesetas) which the Second Republic voted for its first President, Sr. Alcalá Zamora, and the further allowance of £50,000 (1,250,000 pesetas) made to him for expenses. Under the Monarchy, salaries were smaller, but the sums budgeted for expenses were a byword: the Minister for Home Affairs received 1,150,000 pesetas (£46,000); the Minister for Foreign Affairs, 987,000 (£39,480); the Minister of Justice 694,000 (£27,760). In the Prime Minister's department £6,000 (about the total amount of the stipends of four Archbishops) was allotted to lighting and heating, while the wages and expenses of the porters in the Foreign Office came to £1,740 or approximately the stipend of a Cardinal Primate. After these contrasts it is hard to see how anything can be said about the wealth of the hierarchy.

When we come down to canonries we begin to touch something approaching poverty. A Dean receives from 3,750 to 5,000 pesetas (£150 to £200) yearly; a Canon from 2,000 to 4,000 (£80 to £160); a holder of any other benefice not involving the cure of souls, from 750 to 2,000 (£30 to £80). The variations are not due to any periodic increment, for there is no salary scale: a canon at the end of his career is still receiving approximately the stipend of a junior State secondary schoolmaster. They depend upon whether the dignitary is attached to a collegiate church, to the cathedral of a diocese or to the cathedral of an archdiocese. If the life of a canon is one of wealth or poverty let any practical man determine. Genteel poverty advertises little; but a recent writer tells of a Canon of a small cathedral, personally known to him, whose income consists of his annual stipend of 3,600 pesetas (£144 at par; £95 in 1936) with the addition of occasional *estipendios de misa*, totalling not more than a few pounds yearly. On this he, a man of sixty, not only lives but supports two sisters ten and twenty years older than himself.

But the boundary-line of the incredible is reached only when we come to the foot of the ecclesiastical ladder and review the stipends of the parish clergy. The following are the stipends of which the Republican Government of 1931 proposed to deprive their recipients. Of all the incumbents in Spain, barely 50 receive stipends of over £100 per annum; 192 receive from £80 to £100 (and in 24 dioceses there is not an incumbent receiving so much as £80); 1,219 receive from £40 to £80; 10,346 from £28 to £40; 4,630 from £20 to £28; a small number receive even less than £20. It need hardly be said that there is no system of superannuation. These pittances are paid by the State, as will later be seen, as partial compensation for the confiscation of Church property. How the clergy both live and maintain their churches on them only they and their generous parishioners know. Sometimes the payments fall into arrears. Being recruited to a large extent from the lower middle classes, the clergy have very seldom any private means. They have therefore to supplement their stipend by accepting charity or seeking supplementary employment. In the country districts, they make a living out of poultry-farming, keeping goats or selling the produce of allotments. In the towns, they may obtain what with bitter irony could be described in English as "clerical" work. It is not surprising that, with the vast increase in the cost of living, the position of the clergy, even before their miserable stipends

were taken from them, was becoming more and more difficult; that a campaign was in progress for the raising of the
minimum stipend to £40 yearly; and that the number of
ordination candidates was showing a marked decline.

Much more could be said about the poverty of the Church,
but these few pages will suffice to show that any contrary
impression which the visitor to Spain may form is illusory.
Writers of travel-books are always impressed by the splen-
dour of Catholic worship in Spain and by the costliness of
the vestments, plate, pictures, statues and other adjuncts
of worship. But these, of course, are inalienable heirlooms
and even anti-clerical propagandists have never suggested
that any of them are sold (or could conceivably be sold) to
satisfy the pangs of hunger. They are in a true sense
the Church's treasure, for they symbolize the spirit of
worship and devotion which is its greatest gift to God. But
behind its façade of rich heirlooms the Church in Spain is
pitiably poor.

Another criticism of the Church in Spain—again a
criticism made by Catholics as well as Protestants—is that
it has had too much to do with politics.

This charge, as far as the past is concerned, is not without
substance. For myself, I hold that in many countries and
in many ages the spirituality of the Catholic Church has
suffered from the political interventions of the Vatican—
activities often reflected in the internal history of the Church
in those countries. This view is confirmed by the testimony
of numerous historians. In Spain, during the nineteenth
century, the Church, like the Army, was a constant force
in politics, though it is also fair to say that, as we shall see,
spoliation of the Church was a constant theme of political
discussion, so that it would have been difficult for the
Church to remain entirely aloof. At the same time, per-
sonalities like Sor Patrocinio, the fraudulent "nun of the

stigmata," who obtained an ascendancy over Queen Isabel II and her Consort and overthrew Prime Ministers and Governments, did much to bring the Church into discredit and increase the number of anti-clericals. But since at the beginning of the twentieth century the relations between Church and State became stable there has been little or no political activity in the Church—certainly no more than one finds from time to time in the Anglican Church or in the Protestant Nonconformist bodies in this country.[1]

What to my mind has been the principal fault of the Church in Spain—a fault with which it is charged much less often than those already enumerated—is its attitude to progress. In many countries, no doubt, a steady, conservative influence is much to be desired, and for many reasons the Church may act as a suitable restraining force upon hastily formed and ill-considered ideas and innovations. But Spain, during the nineteenth century, was far too nearly isolated from the rest of Europe for her own well-being. All over the continent ideas were advancing and leaving her behind. From being indifferent to European progress she came to glory in her withdrawal from the current of that progress. And so she was content to lag behind much smaller and poorer countries—not only in philosophy and abstract science but in material well-being. Her educational system, the inefficiency of her communications, her insensibility to comfort, to cleanliness and to sanitation reinforced the Black Legend which all over Europe was firmly believed and gave her the reputation of being highly "romantic" and picturesque but in other respects quite impossible.

Now in such fields as education and physical hygiene

[1] It should be unnecessary to recall the activities of the Nonconformist Churches with regard to the Education Act of 1902, their identification of themselves with Liberalism and Liberal measures in the years following the General Election of 1906 and Anglican opposition to the Welsh Disestablishment Act during the same period.

one might have expected the Church to lead. She did not. She followed unenterprisingly in the wake of the sluggish current which nineteenth-century Spain pathetically believed to be progress. One trivial example will serve as a parable. Those who frequented Spanish seaside resorts ten years or so ago may remember that women and girls used to bathe in a long dark two-piece garment with sleeves coming down to the wrist, both the tunic portion and the sleeves being of a voluminousness which defies description. Inside the doors of the churches of these resorts, with a singular lack of humour, had been placed a placard in which a photograph of a girl thus clad, labelled "modest," appeared by the side of a girl attired for bathing in the costume worn in every other country of Europe, labelled "immodest." Either the preference of the young for the latter appellation or the ridiculousness of the mid-Victorian garment drove it completely out of fashion, and to-day girls in Spain bathe, like girls elsewhere, hygienically.

Though trivial, the example is both significant and symbolic. Apply the allegory to all kinds of other customs and ideas and you have the chief fault of the Church in Spain. It was, to use a euphemism, ultra-conservative; blunter critics would describe it as obscurantist and reactionary. The dramatic censor who banned Lope de Vega's comedy *Los Milagros del desprecio* ("Miracles of disdain") on the ground that only God could work miracles was a typical product of the age of Ferdinand VII. Nor was this unintelligent rigidity of attitude all. One of Antonio Machado's characteristically terse judgments on his country as a whole applies with particular force to the Church in Spain during the nineteenth century: *Desprecia cuanto ignora.* "It despised everything that it failed to understand." All forms of science, among conventional and respectable people, tended to be suspect and the less was known of a science the more suspect it was. Foreign ideas and customs had to be looked at very carefully and if there was any suggestion of unconventionality about them they were better left alone: from that point it was only a step to the condemning of them. Going about Spain even now, and talking with religious people—both clergy and laity—one is shocked to find how readily they condemn individuals, ideas and tendencies as atheistic, a word which in this country we use with great care. "Oh, he's an atheist!" is quite a common remark to hear about some person of whose religious beliefs the speaker, on investigation being made, is found to know absolutely nothing. And if this is so to-day, after something like forty years of the most marked progress, what must it have been in mid-nineteenth century?

Some idea can be formed of what it was by reading Leopoldo Alas' novel *La Regenta*, or, better still, the *Doña Perfecta* of Pérez Galdós. The latter novel, published in 1876, is the work of a Liberal polemist who had considerable technical skill as a writer and holds a high place in the history of Spanish fiction. Though it is of course a caricature, one can recognize even to-day how closely its characters resemble portraits.   Orbajosa, the gossiping little cathedral city, makes one shudder; so does Doña Perfecta, the forbiddingly religious lady who represents the characteristic we are describing—a combination of religious fanaticism and lack of culture. Don Inocencio, her confessor and principal ally, is overdrawn and therefore less convincing, as is his nephew, the officious little lawyer, Jacinto. But the theme of the play—the duel between Doña Perfecta and the young engineer Pepe Rey, who is in love with her daughter—is only too eloquent. Pepe has modern ideas and a sane, healthy outlook; the air of Orbajosa stifles him; all the good people point to him as a "Voltairean" and an "atheist." It is above all his devotion to science that they resent: "science calls everything false which is most real; denies the existence of a spiritual life; scoffs at mystic ecstasy;

34

kills faith." Eventually Doña Perfecta plots against him and the story has a tragic, not to say a melodramatic, ending. And not the least tragic aspect of it is that, when her daughter's suitor has lost his life and her daughter has lost her reason, Doña Perfecta herself—"the only person of whom they never speak ill in Orbajosa"—continues to flourish exceedingly.

Anyone who can read this book and make allowances for the element of exaggeration in it will have some conception of the real weakness of the Church in Spain. There is something to be said, however, on the Church's side, not in condonation but in explanation of this tendency. It has been well put by one of the most intelligent of the Church's nineteenth-century champions, a young priest named Balmes, who might have done great things for it had he not died at the age of thirty-eight. "The careful observer," he remarks (though the adjective was superfluous), "will notice that for a long time religious ideas and sentiments in Spain have been of an extremely bellicose character. The reason is not difficult to guess: for eight centuries religion[1] was in actual conflict with Islam." He develops the idea: the Cross was a symbol of battle; bishops and abbots had as much to do with this "holy war" as had kings. As a result, he concludes, this warlike, crusading spirit became permanently allied in Spain with religious sentiment: "Spain was the armed knight guarding the gates of the holy city."[2]

That we can understand—and to understand should be to forgive, the more so as things have greatly changed since the eighteen-seventies. The Church is no longer the enemy of science; indeed, as we shall see, priests will be found among Spain's scientists in no small number. The religious Orders have done a very great deal to further higher education and research. There are open windows now, even in

[1] It should be noted that he uses the word "religion"—not "Catholicism" or "Christianity"—as though Mohammedanism were not a religion.
[2] *Escritos políticos*, Madrid, 1847, p. 176.

Orbajosa.[1] But the Church in Spain has still much to learn of discrimination and tolerance; and especially she needs to discriminate between the various senses of the word which she dislikes most of all—the word "liberalism." Now it is perfectly true that liberalism as a philosophical system and as a theological doctrine has been condemned by the Church as an error, and it is also true that, in the words of a writer whom no one would accuse of excessive sympathy with the Church,

> Spanish "liberalism" has little in common with those convictions which are labelled with the name in Europe. In Spain it is simply synonymous with anti-clericalism.[2]

One might go farther and say that it has been synonymous with an anti-clericalism which has taken the most practical possible form: ever since political liberalism began in Spain, the advent to power of a Liberal Government has meant that the Church has suffered. One could not therefore expect the Church to approve of political liberalism, any more than of liberalism in philosophy and theology. Nor would one expect to find practising Catholics voting for Liberal candidates, though it is to my mind a harsh judgment which declares those who do so to be guilty, "usually," of "mortal sin." But there is another Spanish definition of liberalism and a more relevant one to this discussion: "opposition to absolutism." In this sense it is almost a synonym of democracy.[3] Those who are Liberals in this sense are not, as such, deserving of the condemnation or disapproval of the Church and of religious people, and it is unfortunate that the Church in Spain has not in the past made a surer alliance with them, since they often have her interests at heart. They believe, for example, that the disestablishment of the Church

[1] Though Sr. de Madariaga (*Spain*, p. 221) records that in the very month during which he was writing a book published in 1930, "a local priest and a local mayor in a small Spanish town made a bonfire of all the books of Galdós which had been purchased by the municipal librarian."

[2] Borkenau: *The Spanish Cockpit*, pp. 7–8.

[3] Cf. *Enciclopedia Espasa*, *s.v.* "liberalismo."

will be a source of spiritual strength to it—and there are many non-politically minded Spanish Catholics who think this: in any case, disestablishment has probably come to stay.[1] They believe in toleration of all religious beliefs, freedom of worship, freedom of instruction, universal suffrage, the educational ladder, equality of treatment in law for women and men and freedom of the Press. These are ideals which should command the sympathies of Catholics and which in our own country have won general acceptance. And yet in a popular Spanish exposition of the Catechism[2] one may read that "freedom of conscience, freedom of worship and of the Press" are "false and pernicious forms of freedom,"[3] that freedom of instruction is not only "pernicious" but "absurd,"[4] that "no Catholic may call himself a Liberal,"[5] that it is "a grave sin to subscribe to Liberal periodicals,"[6] and that daily papers, even if neutral politically, which "constantly praise the good points of Liberals, such as their eloquence, character, honesty or patriotism" are "evil and perverse."[7] It can be imagined what type of citizen is being produced by this kind of instruction.

Not long ago an English author unearthed and commented in a pamphlet upon a Spanish work on the Catechism not unlike what just excerpted[8] and a Jesuit Father made a valiant and skilful attempt to meet his criticisms.[9]

[1] The Church would "not be confessional," declared General Franco in his speech of October 1, 1936, but a fresh Concordat would be made with Rome, and this would "respect the national tradition and the religious feelings of the huge majority of Spaniards." "Though the Church is to remain separated from the State," added the late General Mola (January 28, 1937), "since this is in the interests of both, it must be understood that this separation does not imply divorce, but is rather the outward form of a close spiritual partnership."

[2] *El Catecismo de la Doctrina Cristiana* (adapted from the text of Ripalda by P. Felipe Díez Hidalgo, S.J.), Madrid, 1934.

[3] *Op. cit.*, p. 675.   [4] *Op. cit.*, p. 682.   [5] *Op. cit.*, p. 691.

[6] *Op. cit.*, p. 695.   [7] *Op. cit.*, p. 705.

[8] John Langdon-Davies: *The Spanish Church and Politics*, London, 1937.

[9] M. C. D'Arcy, S.J.: "On Liberalism in Spain," in *The Tablet*, November 27, 1937.

In doing so, however, he began by saying: "I admit that some of the answers from the catechism quoted in the pamphlet look over-simple and betray a lack of knowledge of conditions outside Spain." But I am not sure that they do not also betray a lack of understanding of conditions inside Spain. Those who write, or accept, such commentaries fail to realize that there are many broad-minded Catholics, holding political principles to which most English Catholics would subscribe, who would welcome co-operation with the Church if the Church in Spain were more alive to progress. To declare a permanent state of war upon liberalism and all its works because of its admittedly chequered past will only inflame passions on both sides of the conflict indefinitely. To enter into "conversations" with right-wing liberalism with a view to finding a new *modus vivendi* between Church and State would be a source of new strength to a Spain which sorely needs it.

An interesting application of this point of view was put forward not long ago by a not unsympathetic critic, Don Salvador de Madariaga, who would probably himself come into the category just described. If during the Monarchy, he argues, the Church had co-operated loyally with the State in developing purely lay culture, lay opinion, upon the advent of the Republic, would have been much more understanding than it actually showed itself in the drawing up of the Constitution. And if left-wing intellectuals, on their side, had testified their willingness to co-operate in raising the standard of culture within the Church, the Church might well have met them half-way. He then takes one particular example of the lamentable lack of co-operation between Church and State. Notwithstanding the prowess of the Catholic Church in Spain in past ages in the realms of the queen of sciences, the State Universities are completely secularized and there is not a single Faculty of Theology in

the whole of them.[1] As an alumnus of a University which
teaches theology who has spent nearly all his adult life in
another which does not, I can testify how greatly the
Spanish Universities suffer by this secularization. But the
worst sufferer is the Church; for her future ministers, instead
of joining freely, at the most impressionable age, in the life of
a University, are relegated to seminaries, completely cut off
from lay thought and lay ideals, neither themselves leavening
the academic world nor receiving from it that influence
without which the priest is apt to become narrow in his
interests, in his outlook upon life and in his judgments of
his fellows.

All that has been said in this section is perhaps little
more than a complaint that, from first to last, in the period
under survey, the Church in Spain has been essentially
Spanish and that its defects are not so much those of the
Catholic Church as of Spaniards. After all, its faults are
precisely the faults with which, in the late eighteenth century, José Cadalso charged his fellow-countrymen in the
Cartas Marruecas: ignorance of the sciences, lack of intellectual
curiosity and an "empty wordiness" which describes much
pulpit oratory in Spain.[2] And the explanation of some of
them which Balmes gave is the explanation most commonly
given of the exaggerated idealism of the Spaniard. If this
is so, it explains why the only Spanish Catholics who seem
able to understand such criticisms as have here been made
are those who have lived or travelled abroad. Let Sr. de
Madariaga again stand as an example. "The faults of the
Spanish Church," he writes, "and in particular the lack of
culture of the masses that shelter under her mantle, are due,
not to her being Catholic but to her being Spanish. That
is to say, the Spanish Catholic Church, which once, with
Spain, stood at the very summit of religious culture, has
gone the way of the rest of Spain in its lack of culture and

[1] *Anarquía o Jerarquía*, pp. 219, 246.   [2] Cf. p. 45, below.

its decadence."[1] During the five years of the Second Republic there were signs, as we shall presently see, that the Church was attempting to co-operate in a new way with the civil powers and was accepting disabilities which a Liberal *régime* inevitably brought and which one hoped might in time be lightened. Cardinal Gomá, for example, made it very clear that while, as he put it, hunger is no tonic (*no es ningún tónico la falta de pan*), there are advantages in freedom, even coupled with disendowment: freed from State control, the Church would be able to manage her own affairs more efficiently and her ministers would no longer be thought of as State functionaries.[2] Again, though undoubtedly many parishes were too poor to support their own clergy, others were quite capable of doing so, and the new *régime* would compel the financial support of many well-to-do Catholics who, while the Church was a State Church, thought they were doing their full share by paying taxes.

For these and other reasons, a new spirit conducive to collaboration was growing up in Spain under the Republic. Unhappily, the ultimate outcome of Republican rule was not such as to encourage Catholics to attempt collaboration of this kind again. In that part of Spain, indeed, where left-wing extremism has triumphed, the Church has suffered a new and a terrible martyrdom. My great hope for the disestablished Church in Spain under the Republic was that she might both enjoy a revival of spiritual life and grow, in the best and the only true sense, more liberal. My great fear for her now is that, when the sun of civil favour is once more shining upon her, she may relapse into reaction and torpor. But it may well be that, when peace is restored, and the full extent of her martyrdom becomes realized, she

---

[1] *Op. cit.*, pp. 218, 220. The critic goes on to assert that the Church has not participated in the "modest attempt at a renaissance" which began in Spain some fifty years ago. This seems perhaps a little unfair: the Church is surely better in every way to-day than in the eighteen-eighties.

[2] Gomá, *op. cit.*, I, 219–20.

will assimilate something of the spirit of those martyrs, who, called upon, often without preparation, to die for their Faith, responded unhesitatingly, witnessing to it, again and again, in the supreme moment of trial. "When one feels as we do about God and about Spain," exclaimed a young layman before his execution, "it is not hard to know how to die."[1] Perhaps those who are left, sharing this same belief, may find it easier than in the past to know how to live.[2]

By comparison with these criticisms of the Church in Spain all others that one hears are trivial—some of them even childish. But often it is just these that foster prejudice, especially among persons disposed to believe them; they should therefore be briefly referred to.

1. We are told that the Spanish clergy are of a low type, ill-educated, ill-mannered—with "plump and vulgar faces," to quote one polemist[3]—and though this is cancelled by the contradictory charge often brought against them that they are estranged from their people through having been "recruited from amongst the upper classes,"[4] it may be briefly answered.

That the clergy derive largely from the ranks of the people is one of the glories of the Church in Spain, for by the closeness of their contact with those whom they serve they are able to enter into their lives much more intimately than if they were drawn from the leisured classes and the aristocracy. Actually the latest statistics available show that, of 7,401 youths attending theological seminaries in 1935, 6 were noblemen, 115 were "wealthy" (the standard of "wealth" being an income of over 10,000 pesetas: £400 at par; £250 in 1936), and 7,280 were "poor or on the border-line of poverty."[5] It is thus inherently improbable that, as one somewhat

---

[1] *De Rebus Hispaniae*, No. 3. Burgos, June 30, 1938.
[2] See "The Church in Spain, V: The New Vocations," in *The Tablet*, December 10, 1938.
[3] E. Conze, *op. cit.*, p. 27.
[4] *Joint Letter*, p. 29.
[5] *Ibid.*

critical Catholic author suggests, the sufferings of the clergy in the Civil War should have been due to the failure of the Church to be the "friend of the poor" and of "priests in general" to support "the social advancement of the toiling masses."[1] We shall see in a later chapter that the cause of their sufferings was in fact very different.

That many of the clergy—especially of the country clergy —might be better educated is, I think, a just criticism (though few who make it would be capable of testing its truth) and one hopes that in the Spain of the near future the standard of clerical education may rise. The criticism does not apply to the large majority of the regular clergy, many of whom have studied abroad or have been educated either by foreigners or by Spaniards who have absorbed all that is best in foreign culture. Further, criticism of the educational standards of the secular clergy does not prove exactly what foreigners who unintelligently repeat it think it does. The seminaries, of which the upkeep was undertaken by the State under the 1851 Concordat, have been treated as meanly as the parishes. The annual grant given to the Madrid Seminary, for example, was 41,000 pesetas (£1,640); to that of Santiago, 30,000 (£1,200); to most of the remainder, 22,500 (£900), though two received only £400 and one £300.[2] No Church can make bricks without straw. Once ordained, the clergy, receiving starvation wages—and these often in arrears—and of recent years almost entirely dependent on freewill offerings of congregations who may themselves be poor, have had little opportunity of travelling, book-buying or otherwise keeping abreast of education. Hardworked through the decline, already referred to, in the number of ordinations[3] and also

---

[1] M. Mitchell, *Storm over Spain*, p. 59.

[2] Güenechea, *op. cit.*, pp. 19–20.

[3] P. Peiró tells us, for example, that in the archdiocese of Seville there are only 590 priests for 1,400,000 inhabitants, a huge proportion of these inhabitants being Catholics, and not, as would be the case in England, belonging to a large number of denominations.

because of the largeness of the proportion of their flock who practise their religion (Spain not being a country of half-empty churches), they have little free time and no holidays. Again, though the tourist who has visited Madrid, Seville and Granada may think that train services in Spain are excellent, those who really know the country are aware that, especially in mountainous districts, communications of all kinds are bad in the extreme; that in many villages the average inhabitant hardly travels twenty miles outside it in twenty years; and that the lot of the incumbent is very much the same as that of his people. An appointment to a village cure is, as often as not, from the cultural standpoint, a sentence of death: the country parson in Spain has not his little car which will take him, on his periodical "day off," either to the local golf-links or to the nearest large town, with its theatre, concert-hall and library. One needs to live in a small Spanish village for a month or so to realize its isolation. Thus, even if seminary education were improved by one hundred per cent to-morrow, grave obstacles to progress would still remain. Any change must of necessity be slow and can only come by means of other changes which have nothing to do with the Church. Those who complain of the low standard of education among the clergy are apt to forget that the same criticism is applicable to Civil Servants, schoolmasters, lawyers and indeed all but a very small proportion of professional men in Spain.

The statement—if made from first-hand observation— that any type of cleric is ill-mannered could only come from a critic who has either been singularly unfortunate in his Spanish experiences or who is singularly devoid of insight, for standards of courtesy are proverbially high among Spaniards—as much so among the less educated types as among the better educated: the latter fact is axiomatic to all who know Spain. That the clergy have "plump and vulgar faces" is an interesting statement based probably on the genuine observation of someone who was too anxious to attack the Church to notice that it applies equally to a considerable proportion of the laity. Many Spaniards, long before reaching middle age, find themselves, through their diet and sedentary habits, fattened and coarsened, and in walking down any crowded street one can pick out half-a-dozen laymen of whom it can be said: "There goes the monk of fiction!" Even among the foremost lay scholars in Spain there are those who have "plump and vulgar faces": anyone who has studied there could name a few immediately. And one might add, for the information of the tourist-critic, that many Spaniards still visit the barber only once weekly, so that if from the window of his first-class carriage he occasionally espies an unshaven priest he need not find in the fact one more proof that the Church is degenerate.

2. We are told that the churches in Spain are dirty and ill-kept—and so the parish churches (but not the churches of the Orders) often are. To some extent this is also due to their financial position, though it may fairly be replied that if congregations had a passion for well-kept and hygienic churches freewill offerings would soon provide soap and labour. The true cause is rather apathy, which applies by no means only to churches but to all kinds of other public buildings in Spain. This does not, of course, justify the state of the churches but it goes a long way towards explaining it. Everywhere one finds town halls, municipal and provincial offices, secondary schools, universities, libraries and even large hotels where it is impossible to believe that the staircases are ever scrubbed or the walls cleaned and where one would be glad if the ubiquitous and unlovely spittoon were used more freely. I once paid a visit of inspection to a newly built school with the mayor of a large town who expectorated at intervals on the virgin floor as he walked. Nor is that by any means an isolated

experience. Yet in all these respects Spain is improving, not rapidly but very surely. And as town halls improve, so will churches. One only regrets that the Church follows where she should lead—but that is a re-statement of what has been said already.

3. We are told (chiefly by Spanish anti-clericals) that the services and ceremonies of the Church are pompous, unmeaning and far removed from the simplicity commonly associated with Christ's teaching; and that, in particular, Spanish pulpit oratory is bombastic and empty. The first criticism concerns the Catholic Church as a whole: much could be said with regard to it but it must suffice to remark that the Church can provide the simplest services possible for those who desire them. The second criticism is more relevant; and many Spanish Catholics would sympathize with it, especially those who have attended Catholic churches in other countries. But many more insular Spaniards would not. For the truth is that the full-dress sermon in a cathedral or a large city church is a peculiarly Spanish institution. The Spaniard is a natural orator, and, merely from the aesthetic standpoint, delights in oratory. In order to hear a simple sermon, one has to leave the large cities for the villages, and worship among simple folk. However, the fashion may gradually change. P. Francisco Peiró, a reformer in more directions than one, has suggested with salutary bluntness that the clergy might now cease modelling their style on that of French pulpit oratory of the eighteenth century, speak more simply and naturally and preach chiefly on the Gospels, applying their exhortations to their hearers' everyday lives. Something of this kind might very well prove to be one effect of the War upon the pulpit.

4. We are told that most of the Spanish intellectuals of to-day were educated in schools kept by the religious Orders and that many of these have openly attacked and denounced their former educators, while many more have completely

45

flung aside their religion and no longer believe even in God.[1]
The first statement is undoubtedly true; for, when most of
our intellectuals of to-day were young, the schools of the
Orders were almost alone in providing a sound education.
The second and third, however, if accurate, seem quite
irrelevant. Our Lord Himself had twelve chosen disciples.
One of them betrayed Him; one of them denied Him;
and they all forsook Him and fled. Which of His followers
to-day is immune against faithless disciples? The pupil's
defection need cast no stigma upon the teacher. Nor is this
phenomenon unknown in our own country. Many thousands of Englishmen who were educated at public schools
with their daily chapel services and their regular religious
instruction have openly attacked their own schools, or the
public school system, and have completely discarded what
religious faith they ever had. Yet very few critics will be
found to base upon those facts a condemnation of the system.

5. Finally, a very curious argument has been used of
late as a weapon against the Church in Spain—an argument
(or more properly an inference) drawn from the tragic times
through which she has recently been passing. It is inferred
from the very fact that the Church in Spain has suffered so
grievously, that she must in some way have "failed" or been
false to her mission. To this implication any fair-minded
person must take the strongest objection. We do not find
that, in the first days of Christianity, those who were false
to it were martyred but those who were true. We do not
read that Christ ever promised those who followed Him
freedom from persecution: on the contrary, He told them
quite plainly that they might count upon it. But neither
do we find that He promised persecution to those who left
Him or betrayed Him. The words "If they have persecuted
Me, they will also persecute you," the words "Ye shall be
hated of all men for My Name's sake," were spoken by

---

[1] Cf. Moreno, *op. cit.*, p. 16.

Christ to His disciples, not to His enemies. No reiteration of Christ in the Gospels is more striking than that confident future tense: "*When* they persecute you . . .," "They *will* persecute you . . .," "Ye *shall* be persecuted. . . ." Not "may," but "shall." If I am faithful and fearless in my allegiance to Christ, I know that, though I *may* be loved or esteemed in one place, I *shall* be hated or maligned in another. It is no question of possibility but a simple statement of fact.

Now it is quite probable that, though faithful, sincere and courageous, I may also be over-blunt or tactless in my presentation of the faith that is in me, and my enemies may be attacking me, or profess to be attacking me, not for my words but for the manner of them. Or I may, from time to time, fall from my high ideals and my enemies may then take as their target my faults and shortcomings, though it will not be these that have aroused them. But in any case, if over my entire period of discipleship I am going to be faithful, I know that my life will not be an easy one.

So with the Church in Spain. No doubt her enemies can point to faults in her present or her past, to lost opportunities, to unworthy ministers. And, being opposed to her teaching root and branch and anxious to bring all the evidence they can against her, they proffer the facile generalization that she has "failed." But we who have known her for many years, though fully and frankly recognizing what we think to be her deficiencies—and perhaps not always agreeing about these—are united in our defence of her as having faithfully witnessed to God and to the Christian verities, and merited, for her constancy, her conviction and her courage, the hatred and suffering promised her by her Lord. It is not necessarily for his sins, or for the sins of his parents, that the Spanish Catholic has suffered, but rather "that the works of God should be made manifest in him."

CHAPTER II

THE ORDERS, THEIR TRADITION AND THEIR HISTORY FROM 1700 TO 1851

THE INSTINCT which leads Christian people to dedicate themselves to the contemplative life is as old as the instinct which led Mary to leave her sister to her household tasks and choose the "better part" of sitting at the feet of the Master. The instinct which makes them dissatisfied with a mere keeping of the Commandments and arouses within them an illimitable spiritual yearning is as old as the eagerness for perfection of the rich young man who learned from the lips of Christ the hardest lesson ever known. The instinct which prompts them to forsake all they most prize—"houses, or brethren, or sisters, or father, or mother, or wife, or children, or lands"—in order to serve and follow Christ without external impediment is as old as the simple faith of the fishermen who, hearing His call, abandoned their nets without question for a life of hardship which was also a life of service. Renunciation inspired by love and love increased a thousandfold by renunciation have always been characteristics of the Christian religion and wherever he finds them no Christian worthy of the name can fail to accord them recognition and reverence. In individuals of varying temperament and in communities of varying allegiance they have found many and often very dissimilar means of expression. But in the Catholic Church their principal outlet has been the creation of those Orders, Societies, Congregations and other bodies which for the sake of convenience will be described in this book as religious Orders.[1]

[1] An exception is made of the Society of Jesus, the best known of the Congregations which are not technically Orders.

There will always, it is safe to assume, be religious Orders
in the Church, because the religious life satisfies a need of
the Christian soul which in no other way can be wholly
satisfied, and because it is natural, as well as convenient,
that those who devote themselves to that life should seek
each other's company. Let some Government unable to
appreciate Christian ideals dissolve the Orders and their
members will no doubt bow to authority; but if they leave
the country it will be to practise their vocation within a
foreign community, or if they remain it will be to continue
to keep their rule within the inviolable sanctuary of the soul.

It is easy to understand how non-Christians, who know
nothing of the strife of prayer and have no belief in the
efficacy of prayer, can mistake the contemplative's "rest
most busy"—the strenuous and disciplined spiritual life of
the religious—for something hardly distinguishable from
idleness. But the Christian, whether Catholic or Protestant,
should surely know better than this. He should realize,
from his individual experience, what a gain it is for a nation
to have communities of men and women who have flung
aside all worldly ambitions and cut all worldly ties in order
to devote themselves unceasingly to intercourse with God.
He should be able to appreciate the inestimable advantage
which a nation must derive from the leaven of prayer working
within it when one of its inhabitants in every five hundred
or every thousand is a man or woman helping to forge an
unbroken chain of prayer and devoting the hours not so
occupied to labours undertaken on behalf of humanity
without thought or possibility of personal gain.

To have had, through the ages, millions of such dedicated
lives—an immense spiritual force never more potent or more
precious than in these days of unprecedented unrest—has
been the fortunate lot of Spain. It has sometimes been said
that the proportion of religious to the rest of the population
of that country is unduly large and suggested that many of

them must have been prompted by other than spiritual motives since it is unlikely that a vocation for the contemplative life would be given to so many. As a matter of fact, the numbers of Spanish religious have been ridiculously exaggerated by the Church's enemies[1] but even if they were as large as is alleged one can see no justification for the deduction that they are excessive. A country with the age-long traditions of Catholic Spain might be expected to produce more vocations than most others and the Lord's hand is not shortened because we are living in the twentieth century. The decline in the number of religious is no doubt partly due to the fact that there are now more outlets for Christian social service in the world than there were formerly. Partly, too, it may be due to the continued attacks on the Orders, to be described in the following chapters: one effect of these has been to drive numbers of Spanish religious abroad, while another may well have been to dissuade timorous souls from enlisting in the highest kind of service.

The only way in which one can estimate the fitness of religious to follow their high calling is to get to know them, and it is a particularly noteworthy fact that, of the critics, Spanish or foreign, of the Orders, hardly one knows anything about them, as a whole, at first hand. The huge majority merely repeat, and often improve upon, calumnies which they have read, and know less of the Orders even than those who have been educated by one of them. I can at least claim long personal acquaintance with twelve; I have visited them on all kinds of occasions, often unexpectedly and sometimes without even an introduction. Though some of their members, especially those of lowly origin, are persons of no great depth of learning or breadth of culture, others have astounded me by their knowledge of men and things, their encyclopaedic erudition and their scientific outlook. But one and all—I cannot recall an exception—have given

---

[1] Cf. Appendix III, below.

an unmistakable impression of being holy and humble men
of heart, worthy of their high vocation. And in many of
them one can see at a glance that prayer is a reality, and
that they live very near to God.

The abiding glory of the religious Orders in Spain is to
have produced heroes, saints and martyrs in such profusion
that in the course of a brief survey merely to enumerate
them is an impossibility. A few years ago one might have
been tempted to think that heroes, saints and martyrs exist
no longer, or at least, with Menéndez y Pelayo, that they
are less abundant now than in the days of old.[1] There are
even those who have said frequently and openly that the
glory of the Orders has departed since they can no longer
produce such men to-day. But the history of 1936 has
shown that this is not so; once again, as in past centuries,
the Orders, with the secular clergy and the Catholic laity,
have given ample proof of their constancy and courage.
In the course of a persecution the intensity of which has
perhaps never been exceeded in the history of Christianity,
thousands of priests and religious perished "because they
were the chosen servants of Christ." "Of not one of them,"
record the Spanish Bishops, "is it known that he faltered in
the hour of martyrdom; thousands of them gave the highest
examples of heroism. This is the unfading glory of our
Spain."[2]

It is inaccurate, then, to think of the great Spanish saints
as belonging to an age of spiritual valour now closed for
ever. No less worthy of their founders and of their country
are the religious of to-day than were those of the Ages of
Faith: whether, like the Augustinians and the Benedictines,
they have their origins in the early centuries of Christian
history; whether, like the Cistercians, the Carthusians, the
Dominicans and the Franciscans, their Orders were founded
in the Middle Ages; whether, with the Discalced Carmelites,

[1] *Ciencia Española*, Madrid, 1887, I, 191. [2] *Joint Letter*, p. 31.

the Jesuits and the Hospitallers of St. John of God, their societies date from the period of the Counter-Reformation; or whether, like numbers of the smaller congregations, they belong to a later age. All the bodies named, and very many more, have had their saints and their heroes in Spain. Let us try, in a few lines, to form some faint idea of the magnitude of the debt which Christianity owes them.[1]

A convenient starting-point is the birth of St. Dominic in 1170. How many people know that St. Dominic was a Spaniard and that the Order of Preachers is one of our debts to Spain? Santo Domingo de Guzmán is his Spanish name and he was a native of those splendidly encastled heights which we call Old Castile. His seventeen first Preachers bore witness to the quality of mediaeval Spanish sanctity; the Order into which they grew, to the efficiency of mediaeval Spanish organization. Among his followers and their associates are many who have left their mark deep on Spanish history. One of them was St. Ramón Peñafort, an early General of the Order, at whose suggestion St. Thomas is said to have written his *Summa contra Gentiles*. A companion of St. Ramón's, St. Peter Nolasco, founded the Order of St. Mary of Mercy, one of the countless societies inspired by the Spanish instinct of charity, having for its original purpose the ransom of captives taken in the wars against Turks and Moors. In the late fourteenth and early fifteenth centuries another Dominican, St. Vincent Ferrer, bestrides one complete epoch of Spanish history as preacher, philosopher, statesman and saint. In the sixteenth century, Luis de Granada became known as an outstanding preacher, ascetic and mystic, not only in Spain, but also in France and England.

Among the gifts of Spain to the Order of St. Francis are Blessed Ramón Lull, a tertiary who was one of the most

---

[1] This subject I have treated at much greater length in *Our Debt to Spain* (London, 1938). It is therefore only touched upon here.

active of mediaeval missionaries and died a martyr in Africa; St. Peter Regalato, the gentle reformer of the fifteenth century; St. Diego of Alcalá, who evangelized the Canary Islands; St. Francis Solano, the "Apostle of South America"; and St. Peter of Alcántara, author of that "Golden Book" known as the *Treatise of Prayer and Meditation* and the friend and counsellor of St. Teresa. Other Franciscan mystics, such as Bernardino de Laredo, Francisco de Osuna and Juan de los Ángeles, would be considered of the first rank at any other time than the sixteenth century and in any other country than Spain.

The Augustinians give us a galaxy of mystics—Bernardo Oliver, Alonso de Orozco, Pedro Malón de Chaide, Luis de León and many more. They have also one great world-figure—St. Thomas Villanueva, "Father of the Poor," who during his last illness gave away even the very bed on which he was lying and used to say that he could call nothing his own but the obligation to distribute to his brethren the possessions with which God had entrusted him.

A few years after St. Thomas' death the Discalced Rule of the Carmelite Order came into existence as the work of one of the greatest women in the history not only of Spain but of the entire world, St. Teresa. Inflexible and indomitable of purpose, she was another child of stern Castile who inherited the temperament of her mother. At the same time, as we know from her extant letters, there was never a saint of outlook more completely human. The achievement of her numerous foundations pales only before her conquests in the spiritual life, for she is one of the greatest contemplatives of all time. Hardly second to her comes her disciple, a member of the same reformed Order, St. John of the Cross, Doctor of the Church Universal and one of the greatest poets of Spain, but before all else a mystic. His *Ascent of Mount Carmel, Dark Night of the Soul, Spiritual Canticle* and *Living Flame of Love* are among the greatest mystical treatises to have been written since the time of the early Fathers.

From the contemplative type we pass to the active in recalling the lives of the first members of the Society of Jesus. This body was founded, in 1538, by a Spaniard, St. Ignatius of Loyola, a soldier wounded in battle at the age of thirty, who, after overcoming incredible difficulties, executed an idea conceived soon after his conversion—the creation of a Society whose members would be ready to go anywhere and do anything *ad maiorem Dei gloriam*: "for the greater glory of God."

With St. Ignatius, in 1622, were canonized three other Spanish saints: St. Isidro, Patron of Madrid, St. Teresa and St. Francis Xavier. The last of these was one of the original members of St. Ignatius' Society, one of the most devoted and self-sacrificing of all the saints, often described as the greatest missionary since St. Paul. He worked, with an efficiency hardly less remarkable than his Christ-like abnegation, in India, Ceylon, Japan, China, the Moluccas, and many another outpost of the Far East. The principal sphere of the third General of the Society, St. Francis Borgia, was Spanish America. St. Peter Claver spent nearly forty years working among negro slaves in the West Indies.

Perhaps the best way to form an opinion of the heroic activities both of the Society of Jesus and of the various Orders whose Spanish members entered the mission-field is to read the early history of Spanish America.[1] There were the Franciscans who went with Narváez to Florida and all of whom apparently lost their lives; the Franciscans who evangelized Texas, notably Fray Andrés de Olmos, who spent his life there; the two early groups of Dominicans in Florida, nearly all of whom were killed; the more successful expedition of Jesuit missionaries sent to Florida and Mexico by St. Francis Borgia; the Franciscans martyred in New

[1] Cf. *Our Debt to Spain*, pp. 89–132.

54

Mexico; the Dominican, Franciscan and Jesuit missions in Mexico and Lower California; and very many more. No sooner did one of these missionaries lose his life than two more went out in his place. We have to honour alike the known and the unknown, for all alike left their motherland and went out they knew not to what, for Christ's sake and the Gospel's.

These few paragraphs will indicate the lines of a reply to any suggestion that the religious Orders were degenerate when their members were most numerous, *i.e.*, in the ages of Spain's greatest prosperity. It would be an attractive task to enter in greater detail into the history of the four centuries which are continuously illumined by Spanish saintliness. But, as the object of this book is to discuss the immediate past and the present, we must take up the history of the Church and the Orders in more recent times.

The history of the religious Orders in Spain during the eighteenth and nineteenth centuries, largely a history of spoliation and persecution, is not completely separable from that of the Church in Spain as a whole. As we trace the one, we shall have continually to glance at the other and we shall find the same motive forces behind both. These are four in number, which in approximately chronological order may be set out as follows:

1. Desire of the King for control in ecclesiastical matters (eighteenth century).

2. Eagerness of the State to acquire the wealth of the Church—due primarily to the impoverishment of the country (eighteenth and nineteenth centuries).

3. Anti-clericalism; or dislike and distrust of the clergy and the part which they played, or were alleged to have played, in the life of the country (nineteenth century; continuing, with varying intensity, in the twentieth).

4. Development of what is often broadly termed "Communism": *i.e.*, a number of related but not identical

proletarian movements, one common factor of which is disbelief in, and denial of, God (late nineteenth and twentieth centuries).

We shall see how the first two motives gradually disappeared, how the third slightly decreased, and how the fourth, in recent times, has greatly increased in importance.

If we were to go back far enough, to the Middle Ages, we should find that the earliest motive of the four was the second. Before the Union of the Kingdoms it was common enough for necessitous kings to take "loans" from the Church, which might or might not be repaid, and even the Catholic Monarchs, when short of money for their wars, would help themselves to Church plate, though it is fair to say that they had the reputation of invariably restoring its value. It was with the Hapsburgs, the last of whom died in 1700, and still more markedly with the Bourbons, that the first motive became prominent; and, curiously enough, before the end of the eighteenth century, despite the increasing poverty of the country, and the fact that members of religious Orders were far more numerous in proportion to the population than they are to-day, neither the Orders nor the Church as a whole suffered greatly through spoliation. When the State needed the financial aid of the Church, it either found that the Crown (reinforced by leading theologians) was an effective Defender of the Faith, or, on occasions, combined with the Crown to obtain the necessary aid by arrangement with the Vatican. Philip II, the worst offender among the Hapsburg kings, planned expropriations on a considerable scale but put few of them into practice and in his will ordered the return to the Church of anything he had taken from it.

It was when, even in "the most Catholic country of Europe," the influence of the Age of Enlightenment began to be felt that the Church first met with serious difficulties.

Its conflict with the State, paralleled in several other countries, turned principally on the question of royal prerogative. As a secondary issue came the desire of the State, which supported this prerogative, to own the wealth and property of the Church, and especially that of the Orders. This, at one time considerable,[1] included also at one time a great deal of land allowed to remain idle, a fact which brought economists on to the side of the State, but which was for long thought to be sufficiently well met by a prohibition, under the early Bourbons, of the transference of real estate to mortmain. It was unhappily as the Orders began to devote more of their wealth to educational and philanthropic work, which they have done increasingly for generations, that the growing poverty of the country began to make the temptation to enrichment by confiscation irresistible. Nor was this procedure without some show of justification. There were arguments—such as that of the economists—which were sufficiently plausible to stifle the consciences even of those who set store by Christian principles and would have been shocked by such theories, now used to defend spoliation, as that the State is the sovereign owner of all property, while the nominal holders have only the use of it, and that consequently the State can forbid any kind of body to hold property or can dissolve the body and confiscate the property. To most people at that time such ideas would have seemed, as to many they still seem, the babble of criminals, and they would have looked upon spoliation as an offence properly punishable by imprisonment. They knew that the right of the Church to hold property like any other corporation is inherent in its nature, and that, in Spanish history, the recognition of this right goes back, through the *Siete Partidas* of Alfonso X, to the seventh-century Fuero Juzgo.

---

[1] On the extent and nature of ecclesiastical property before the end of the eighteenth century, see H. Butler Clarke, *op. cit.*, pp. 5–6.

On the question of the royal prerogative, it became clear when in 1700 the Bourbons, with their well-known absolutist tendencies, succeeded the Hapsburgs, that a long conflict was in sight. For almost half the eighteenth century Spain was ruled by the first of the dynasty, Louis XIV's grandson, Philip V; and both he and his immediate successors challenged every possible ecclesiastical prerogative, especially in the matter of patronage. The support given by the Vatican to Philip's rival, the Archduke Charles of Austria (afterwards the Emperor Charles VI), whose candidature to the throne caused the War of the Spanish Succession, made relations between Church and King even more difficult: though it should be noted, with regard to this, that a proposal made by Macanaz in 1713 to levy certain exactions on the Church in order to pay for the War was unsuccessful. The War ended, negotiations for an agreement began. The first attempt at a Concordat, drawn up by Clement XII and Philip V in 1737, pleased neither clericals nor regalists. The second, made in 1753, between Ferdinand VI and Benedict XIV, was more effective. With certain exceptions, and in exchange for a large indemnity paid to the Holy See, all ecclesiastical patronage was made over to the Crown. This settled one of the most burning questions at issue but left others which, during the reign of Charles III (1759–88), became more pressing. Charles's ministers were for the most part regalists; some of them, too, were in close touch with French encyclopaedism. So minor clashes between Church and State occurred continually; the expropriation of Church property began to be talked of; and in many ways the King attempted, with some success, to tighten his hold upon the clergy.[1]

At this stage there comes into the foreground of the picture the Society of Jesus, very powerful both in Spain and abroad but surrounded also by powerful enemies—

[1] Altamira, IV, 216–17.

Jansenists, Protestants and free-thinkers—and not always too kindly looked upon either by the religious Orders or by the secular clergy. For a century and a half there had been conflicts between this or that Order and the Jesuits, sometimes on doctrinal issues, sometimes on matters of ecclesiastical polity, and, the Pyrenees being (in Louis XIV's phrase) no more, the war which raged around Pascal's *Lettres Provinciales* was not without its repercussions in Spain. The Spanish Universities, too, which, since the Golden Age, had sadly decayed, were envious of the efficiency and well-merited popularity of the colleges belonging to the Jesuits, who have always been notably successful as teachers.[1] The fact that both Philip V and Ferdinand VI had Jesuit confessors gave the Society unique political opportunities, which were increased as they gained virtual control of the still existent Inquisition.[2] Frequent clashes, together with the rapid influx of ideas and sentiments often loosely described as "Voltairean," led up to a crisis which was ended, in 1767, by the expulsion of the Jesuits from Spain. In 1759, through the influence of the despotic Pombal, the Society had been dissolved in Portugal, and, three years later, despite episcopal opposition, the long struggle in France had ended in its suppression by Louis XV. In 1773 the triumph of the Society's opponents was completed by the Papal brief *Dominus ac Redemptor*, which suppressed it entirely. Only in 1814, when the worst of the storms which in the interval had passed over Europe had subsided, was it re-established.

It is more difficult to pronounce upon the justice and prudence of the expulsion of the Jesuits from Spain than upon attacks made on them later and one's judgment is apt to be unduly influenced by the circumstantial accounts of how their *residencias* were surrounded by troops, and they

---

[1] Altamira, IV, 224.
[2] Further details will be found in Altamira, IV, 223–9.

themselves evicted by force, and, without regard to sickness or age, hustled out of the country. But it may at least be said that such action seems to have been almost inevitable if the situation was to be eased and that it was certainly popular with many who were in no way hostile to religion.[1] Further, although the property of the Society was sequestrated, it was expressly laid down that in its disposition regard should be had to the canons of the Church, to the wishes of founders, to the honour of Divine worship, to the salvation of souls and (last in order, it will be observed) to public utility.[2] It did not therefore go to provide anti-religious teaching—or to found museums!

Regalism, as such, died out with the eighteenth century. In the nineteenth it occasionally reappeared—and it was condemned, with liberalism, in the Syllabus of 1864—but it was no longer the force which it had been earlier. The poverty of the country, however, now brought the second of our motives into the foreground. The precedent set by Charles III proved an unfortunate one. The suppression of the Society of Jesus, said his successors, had provided the State with some useful property and the religious Orders could be made to yield fruit of equal value. So, in 1798, under Charles IV, the first measure of expropriation, in the modern sense of that word, passed into law, authorizing the confiscation and sale of the real estate belonging to religious brotherhoods, charitable institutions, establishments of pious foundation and benefices under lay patronage and giving the owners three per cent Government bonds as compensation. No reference was made to Rome until after the law had been passed. In 1805 the King asked and obtained from the Pope permission to sell, against similar compensation, Church property producing income to the value of £64,000 sterling per annum. The step, however,

---

[1] Cf., for example, the views of the Augustinian historian, P. Miguélez, *op. cit.*, pp. 327 ff.
[2] Altamira, IV, 239.

was not a successful one; for the sales were so badly managed that, when only one-quarter of the property had been disposed of, a generally felt dissatisfaction caused their suspension.

Further confiscations on a smaller scale and occasional suppressions of benefices are recorded during the reign of Charles IV; but it was upon Napoleon's invasion of Spain, which followed Charles's abdication, that the religious Orders began to be attacked in earnest. One of Napoleon's first acts was to decree the reduction of the religious houses by two-thirds; and his brother Joseph (August 18, 1809) amplified this "liberal programme"[1] by suppressing them all. He then seized their property, to say nothing of plate, vestments and anything else of value which he could find, and appropriated the whole for the Treasury. These decrees, even in the invaded provinces, were resisted to the utmost. There were murders—there were even occasional atrocities. The Bishop of Coria, an old man of eighty-five, was dragged from his bed by Soult's troops and shot. General Palafox's confessor, an Escolapian named P. Basilio Boggiero, was murdered and his dead body flung into the Ebro. After the battle of Uclés, the convent standing above the town was sacked by the French; the cathedral of Solsona was burned down; and friars were shot at Sagunto and Castellón.

For these and other outrages there was, from the French point of view, this degree of justification—that the war against Napoleon was an uprising of the entire population of Spain and that not only was it approved by the hierarchy as whole-heartedly as though it had been a religious crusade but parish priests attended patriotic recruiting meetings and it was even said that monks had left their cloisters to help arouse lethargic villagers to fight for their country. Charles IV's son, who later came to the throne as

[1] Mesonero Romanos, cit. Menéndez y Pelayo: *Historia de los Heterodoxos Españoles*, VII, 13.

Ferdinand VII, was idealized by clergy as much as by laity. "Ferdinand the Desired" was the name they gave him, and one and all were confident that he would justify his name. Unfortunately he did quite the contrary, and, despite the assiduity with which he supported the Church, clerical writers are outspoken in condemnation of his life and character.

In any case, the Church had first to reckon with the Cortes, which in 1812 brought in the famous Constitution of Cádiz. The Bonaparte decrees suppressing religious houses now became null and void, but spoliation of any kind, especially when directed against those unable to resist it by force, soon grows into a tradition. These Cortes were not fighting against religion as such. Their law embodying the new Constitution began with the words: "In the Name of the Father, of the Son and of the Holy Spirit"; the Constitution itself declared that the national religion "is and will for ever be the Catholic, Apostolic and Roman religion, which alone is true"; and one of their acts was to declare St. Teresa co-patron of Spain with the Apostle St. James. Nevertheless, they treated the Church little better than Napoleon had done. They forbade the making of appeals for money to be devoted to the rebuilding of religious houses which had been destroyed during the invasion; they confirmed the appropriation to the State of the property of all such houses which the invaders had suppressed; and they themselves suppressed all houses which had fewer than twelve inmates, except in any town or village where no other existed, in which case the number of its inmates would be made up to twelve. The distress caused by this measure, added to that which had resulted from the French invasion, can well be imagined. In some parts of the country, homeless and penniless friars were going from one village to another, begging their bread. But, though cases of this kind were brought to the notice of the Cortes, their "Liberal" fervour was in no way diminished. The Papal Nuncio protested against their actions, and was expelled from Spain—"to the accompaniment," says a notably sober historian, "of Liberal applause."[1] Protesting Bishops, too, were exiled or suspended.

These measures, with others equally severe affecting the secular clergy—all of them aiming simply at converting ecclesiastical wealth to secular uses[2]—were at once annulled by Ferdinand VII in 1814 on the restoration of the Bourbons. The suppressed monasteries and convents were reopened and Church property which had been sequestrated was returned to its former owners (May 21, 1814). In the following year (May 29, 1815), after "many and continuous representations from provinces, cities, towns and villages," the Jesuits were allowed to return.[3] So the pendulum began to swing which has been the curse of Spain ever since and which unhappily has gathered much momentum since the end of the War of Independence. Do the opponents of the Church defend those who laid violent hands on Church property by pointing to abuses in its administration? So be it. Abuses there undoubtedly were; but had they been considered by both parties in a spirit of mutual tolerance they might have been satisfactorily solved. As it was, intolerance on the one side led to intolerance on the other. What had originally been in the main a struggle for power between Church and King became a struggle for property. In the course of this transformation, fresh and vehement

---

[1] Pío Zabala: *Historia de España*, I, 201. Cf. Menéndez y Pelayo, *Heterodoxos*, VII, 80–2.

[2] Chiefly: the suspension of elections and appointments to sees and other dignities; the appropriation by the State of the incomes of these offices; the seizure of the funds of various charitable bodies; the confiscation of all Church plate, jewels, etc., not actually being used in public worship; the sequestration of the property of the military Orders and of the Order of St. John of Jerusalem; and the application of certain ecclesiastical dues to the redemption of the Public Debt. On account of the change of *régime*, not all these projects were carried out, as will be gathered from what follows. (Cf. *Heterodoxos*, VII, 84.)

[3] *Op. cit.*, VII, 101–2. The Society of Jesus, suppressed in 1773, had been re-established by Pius VII on August 7, 1814.

fires were kindled. Anti-clerical prejudice became, as we shall see, anti-religious passion. In one sense, the Orders were the victims of these; in another, the chief victim was Spain.

In 1820 occurred the armed revolt against Ferdinand's rule headed by Rafael Riego: this was the first of a long series of attempts to obtain political ends by means of insurrection and it is instructive to note that the initiators of these military revolts were the Liberals. The nature of their "liberalism" may be deduced from the fact that they began by re-expelling the Jesuits (August 14, 1820) and then forced the King, against his will, to sign a decree attacking the religious Orders (October 25), threatening him with further revolution if he vetoed it, as he was entitled to do by the Constitution. In the end, for the sake of peace, he yielded, but retired to his residence at El Escorial as a sign of protest.

So deplorable was Spain's financial plight at this time that to many a raid of Church wealth seemed quite a patriotic enterprise. It was certainly carried out with thoroughness. Many Orders, including those of St. Augustine and St. Benedict, were suppressed altogether; the establishment of any new Order was forbidden; and all religious houses unable to show a minimum of twenty-four professed members were closed. These provisions, which resulted in the disbanding of more than half the religious in the country, effected the secularization of a large amount of entailed Church property. In addition must be recorded the confiscation of half the income received from tithe, the suppression of the military Orders and the closing of the Hospitals of St. John of God; the suspension (April 7, 1821) of all benefices and chaplaincies not conveying the cure of souls; the reduction of the number of parish priests; and the prohibiting of the conferment of major orders (April 26, 1821). Finally, a decree dated November 15, 1822, suppressed all religious houses situated in uninhabited country or (with the exception of the monastery of San Lorenzo del Escorial) in villages of less than 450 inhabitants.

Attempts were also made by these Liberals to obtain the approval and authority of the Church for the Constitution of 1812, which was the *point de départ* for most of their new legislation. By a decree dated April 24, 1820, the Bishops were ordered to have the Constitution proclaimed and expounded by the parish priests from their pulpits, on every Sunday and Holy Day. This they were to do "as part of their obligations, pointing out at the same time the advantages which it brings to all classes in the State and repelling the calumniatory accusations by means of which ignorance and malice have attempted to discredit it."[1] It will be observed that Liberals in Spain have no objection to the preaching of politics by the clergy provided it is Liberal politics.

To so iniquitous a decree there was naturally considerable resistance. One Bishop, at least, who refused to obey it— Don Simón López, Bishop of Orihuela—was expelled from the country. Soon he was joined in exile by the Archbishops of Tarragona and Valencia, and by the Bishops of Oviedo, Minorca, Tarazona, Barcelona, Pamplona and Ceuta. Deeds of violence now began to be reported from many parts of the country. Among these were the assassination of a priest, Don Matías Vinuesa, in Madrid, and demonstrations against, and even personal attacks upon, the Archbishop of Valencia and the Bishop of Barcelona before they were exiled. On November 17, 1822, twenty-four monks, priests and other inhabitants of Manresa were taken out into the country between that city and Montserrat, and there murdered; while, on April 16, 1823, Fray Ramón Strauch, Bishop of Vich, an old man of 75, was led from the city at the bayonet-point with a lay attendant, after which both were shot *por quererse fugar*—i.e., on a pretext, familiar

[1] *Heterodoxos*, VII, 113, n.

to all students of Spanish history, that they were attempting to run away. At Corunna, just over three months later—on the night of July 24, 1823—fifty-one persons, including monks and clergy, were bayoneted and thrown into the sea.

These and other events of the time seem to take us somewhere near the source of the anti-clericalism which became such a feature of Spanish life in the following century. The words "somewhere near" are used advisedly, for no doubt it could theoretically be traced back a century farther, but not in precisely the same form. Henceforward the motive behind successive spoliations of the Church was not merely the desire to find financial aid for a sorely impoverished State: this still persisted, but with it was increasingly mingled the desire to attack the Church for the sake of so doing. As one reads accounts of the parliamentary debates during the Liberal triennium (1820–3), one finds this anti-clerical spirit pervading all the speeches of the Liberal deputies—in the idea, to quote one of them, that the Church was "an army, with prelates for its generals and for its reinforcements the Inquisition"[1]—an army, of course, against which the Liberals must fight.

We must pause for a moment to enquire the reason for this enmity. For the clergy and religious were, as they still are, the best friends of the Spanish people. At this very period of which we are speaking, the clergy of Catalonia had performed the most heroically devoted services during a widespread epidemic of yellow fever. The development of feeling against them among a section of the people seems to have arisen from their militant attitude to the liberalism of the years following 1812. When they had spurred on the people to fight against the French invader they had been acclaimed as good patriots and good citizens: none had protested against them save the *afrancesados*—the "Frenchified ones"—who were held in general contempt. But it

[1] *Heterodoxos*, VII, 114, n.

was not merely because the French were invading Spain that they led the crusade against them; it was because these invaders stood for the "errors of 1789"—that is, for a series of principles of foreign origin, based, as they held, upon premises contrary to the basic doctrines of Christianity.

So, when the Liberals came into power and attempted to force them to preach a political creed which they regarded as fundamentally irreligious, they naturally transferred their opposition from Napoleon to the Liberals. No doubt their outlook was narrow—but after all they were barely twenty years distant from the horrors of the French Revolution, and if we think of modern parallels we can well understand their attitude. And the militancy of the Liberals, as all fair-minded people who read the detailed history of the period will agree, was such as to provoke reprisals.

But it must not be forgotten that then, as a century later, there were clergy and religious on both sides of the conflict. Anti-clericals in Spain delight to make play with the fantastic picture of Fray Antonio Marañón, the Trappist monk, who, with crucifix in one hand and whip in the other, scaled the walls of Seo de Urgel at the head of his "Apostolic" army to recapture it for the King and set up within it a Royalist Regency, one member of which was the Archbishop of Tarragona. But against this picture must be placed the soberer one of the meeting of the Liberal Cortes of 1822, no less than twenty-six members of which were priests. Despite the Church's disapproval of Spanish liberalism, there have always been priests and Catholic laymen sympathetic with it and willing to overlook both its principles and its excesses in favour of what they found in it of good.

The Liberal *régime* inaugurated by Riego's insurrection proved to be a short one. At the end of three years, the victorious march of the French army—the "hundred thousand sons of St. Louis"—gave Ferdinand absolute power again; the *status quo ante* was restored; and scarcely more than three months were needed to undo the anti-religious work of as many years. Each time the pendulum swung, however, passion lent it a slight additional impetus and the excesses of the last ten years of Ferdinand's reign far exceeded those of the preceding triennium.

With his death, in 1833, came a new reaction. First, civil war broke out between the supporters of his infant daughter Isabel, who ascended the throne, and those of his brother, Don Carlos, who claimed it. The struggle was more than a dynastic one: the Carlists, whose cradle and spiritual home is in traditionalist Navarre, represented the *ne plus ultra* of militant Catholic conservatism, as they do to-day. Their war was to them a religious war, as later in the eighteen-seventies and later still in the nineteen-thirties; and they identified, and still identify, religion with politics —to an extent seldom seen elsewhere.[1]

The fact that many, though not all, of the clergy favoured the Carlist cause made this a particularly suitable time for Governments to plunder the Church, while the poverty-stricken state of the country made any such measure once more a tempting one. But before plans were put into action mob violence again broke out, and, allowed as it was to go unchecked and unpunished, proved to be the precursor of much more during the hundred years following. To some extent, no doubt, this was caused by the popular identification of the Church with Carlism; to some extent it was due to the passions roused by the recent political reaction. The mobs—abetted, it is said, by political progressives— found a pretext for directing their fury against the defence-less monks and nuns in the widely spread report that an outbreak of cholera in the summer of 1834 had been caused by monks poisoning wells. Absurd as the story was, it

[1] It would be interesting, but irrelevant to the main purpose of these chapters, to enter into the history of Carlism. The reader is referred to the three articles by A. A. Parker in *Studies*, cited in the Bibliography, below.

sufficed to kindle the flames. In one part of the country after another went up the cry of *¡Mueran los frailes!* "Death to the monks!"

The Jesuits, as usual, bore the brunt of the extremists' fury. Early in the afternoon of July 17, 1834, their college of San Isidro in Madrid was attacked by a mob which called loudly for its inmates' lives. The whole community assembled in their chapel and defended themselves there, but the stand cost fifteen of the defenders their lives, among them four priests of the Society, one of these, P. Juan Artigas, Spain's leading Arabist. Next, the Dominican monastery of Santo Tomás, in the Calle de Atocha, was stormed; and the monks were attacked, and many of them killed, while they were reciting the evening office. At the Mercedarian monastery, in the Plaza del Progreso, eight monks and a lay brother were murdered, including the Provincial, who at the moment of the attack was saying his prayers in choir. Finally, as night fell, the mobs assaulted the friary of San Francisco el Grande. Here a guard had been placed and the friars had believed themselves to be safe. But, just as they had finished their evening meal and were about to go to bed, the doors crashed in, and mobs swarmed into cloister, chapel and refectory. Some of the friars escaped over the walls; the remainder were hunted from room to room and slaughtered. The soldiers—few no doubt and powerless against the crowds—merely looked on at the sight. Figures of the casualties differ, but the most conservative estimate gives the number of friars killed as eighteen and the number of laymen as twenty-three.[1]

These outrages all occurred in one day in the capital of Spain and the seat of its Government. And (in 1834, as later in 1931) the Government did nothing. Not only did the Captain-General allow the riots to continue for five hours before ordering out his soldiers, but no punishment

---

[1] *Heterodoxos*, VII, 223–6.

was meted out to the ringleaders, save that one man was executed—for theft! The outrages themselves were bad enough, but the acquiescence of the Liberal Government in them was worse. Nothing previously had so much exacerbated Catholic feeling; a recent writer has gone so far as to attribute to it the opening of "the great gulf . . . between the old Spain and the new."[1]

A century ago the transit of news was slow and uncertain, but it was inevitable that, sooner or later, the impunity attending these riots should lead to repercussions in the provinces. These began in April 1835 at Saragossa and were continually repeated during the summer. On the first outbreak, gangs paraded the streets shouting "Death to the Archbishop! Death to the Chapter!" but on that occasion they assassinated only two monks, two secular priests and a Franciscan lay brother. Three days later there were similar disturbances at Murcia: here three religious were killed and eighteen wounded and the Bishop, his palace sacked and burned, had to flee. On July 22 Franciscan and Carmelite houses were destroyed at Reus. Three days later took place the worst of all the outbreaks —that of Barcelona. In the initial attack, eighteen religious were killed and the houses of Carmelites, Dominicans, Augustinians and Trinitarians were burned to the ground. All over the city churches were sacked and profaned, libraries dispersed or burned and the dead bodies of religious stripped and mutilated. Here, more than anywhere, passion ran riot: even women, the historians tell us, helped in the destruction of the friaries. At the end of July the flames broke out again, this time at Murcia, and four religious houses—Santo Domingo, San Francisco, La Trinidad and La Merced—were destroyed. "Let us burn the nests," was the cry here, "and the birds will never return." Further riots took place, during this period of

[1] Parker: *The Catholic Church in Spain*, etc., p. 13.

nearly four months, in Tarragona, Valencia, Majorca, Málaga and Salamanca. Hundreds of religious houses were wholly or partially destroyed by fire; hundreds of priests and laymen were killed; hundreds of works of art lost for ever.[1]

And still the Government of the day did nothing! Who can be surprised if many, connecting these unprovoked outrages with the political attacks on the Church made at the same time by the Liberals, began to think of liberalism as of one of the deadly sins, and if to the cry of ¡Mueran los frailes! they responded with a no less sincere one of ¡Mueran los liberales!

In June 1835, after a short and unsuccessful period of government by the political party known as the Moderates, an advanced Liberal, Count Toreno, took office. From this moment a campaign against the Church, prompted jointly by anti-clericalism and the need for replenishing the Treasury, began in earnest. Toreno lost no time in once more dissolving the Society of Jesus and in seizing its property. Three weeks later he decreed the suppression of all religious houses except those having twelve or more inmates (two-thirds of them professed) with the further exception of the houses of missionary congregations and of Escolapians. This rule affected no less than nine hundred religious houses. It was during the passing of these measures that the last of the riots already referred to took place— notably those in Barcelona, where the flames kindled in literal fact by the mobs spread, in a metaphorical sense, much more widely than either they or those who encouraged them could have imagined. When religious houses had been sacked and the clergy had been murdered, the outbreak took on a frankly political character. The military governor was killed; an extremist group seized power in the city; and a bourgeois *junta*, representing the whole of Catalonia—

---

[1] *Heterodoxos*, VII, 227–31; La Fuente, VI, 217–20.

an eminently bourgeois region—set itself up to function until various political demands and grievances should be attended to. The repercussion of these events caused further political riots in Madrid and sporadic outbreaks elsewhere. Before long, Toreno was out of office.

He was succeeded by a wealthy financier named Mendizábal,[1] a man of vehemently Liberal opinions who had taken part in the 1820 rising, had been for many years a political exile in London, and, in June 1835, had been called to Madrid by Toreno as his Finance Minister. Mendizábal was a political opportunist whose path was barred by no excess of scrupulosity. His aim was to confiscate the whole of the property of the Church with the least possible delay; and when, on September 15, 1835, he succeeded Toreno as Prime Minister, he saw the way cleared for the accomplishment of his aim. Less than a month sufficed him to pacify the greater part of the country. Then, on October 11, lest there should be fresh outbreaks before the necessary legislation could be prepared, an emergency decree suppressed all monasteries, save those of the Escolapians and others devoted to the teaching of poor children, those of St. John of God and others who ministered to the sick, and any whose work was to train missionaries for the Philippines. Determined attempts were made to disband even the teaching Orders—notwithstanding the state of Spanish education. The Escolapians, said one deputy, "were not in harmony with the present epoch." The life of nuns—even of teaching nuns—said another, was "anachronistic, absurd and contrary to reason, nature and the spirit of the age."[2] It did not apparently occur to either that the fault might be in the present epoch and the spirit of the age rather than in these men and women who had devoted their lives to the service of God and their fellows.

[1] His true name was Juan Álvarez Méndez but he changed his second (*i.e.*, maternal) name to Mendizábal, and by this he is always known.
[2] Antequera: *La Desamortización*, etc., p. 189.

After surviving a number of purely political vicissitudes, Mendizábal played his trump card in the game of using the Church to re-finance the impoverished country. Three decrees, promulgated on February 19 and March 5 and 9, 1836—anticipated in January by the Civil Governor of Madrid, who forcibly expelled any religious remaining in the capital—popularized the blessed word *desamortización*.[1] By the first of these decrees the whole of the real estate belonging to religious communities was seized and put up for sale—with the object of reducing the enormous public debt, and, as the preamble to the decree put it, of "bringing to Spain animation, life and prosperity" by "creating a copious family of proprietors."[2] By the second and third, all monasteries throughout the country were suppressed. and the number of convents was drastically diminished. No more novices were permitted to enter convents and no two houses of the same Order might exist in one town.

This vindictive measure was not only morally scandalous —it was also unspeakably foolish. It lent the pendulum a new and violent impetus; it perturbed the devout and moderate majority of the people; it drove from their homes thousands of monks and nuns whom the State had to feed or allow to starve; and it also threw on the State many times that number of destitute people for whom the monks and nuns had cared at their Orders' cost. Besides being foolish, the measure proved also to be ineffective, and its results are generally allowed to have been disastrous. They consisted, says Butler Clarke, in "vast gains to a few bold speculators," "scanty profit to the State, huge frauds at the sales, worse confusion in the financial departments, and the creation of titles to real estate which were sure to be called in question."[3] It had been decreed that the confiscated property should be

[1] *I.e.*, the seizure of property held in mortmain (whence the term: the rigidity of the grasp of a "dead hand" is of course proverbial) and the transference of it, as it were, to general circulation.

[2] *Heterodoxos*, VII, 240.   [3] Butler Clarke, *op. cit.*, p. 118.

sold by public auction; and any competent layman, not wholly blinded by prejudice, must have seen that, with so much for sale and with the impossibility of fixing high reserve prices, the proceeds could not be expected to bring great wealth to the Treasury.[1] Those who would gain were sure to be speculators on the look-out for bargains. No "copious family of proprietors," then, was created; in the long run, the chief social outcome of this Liberal legislation was to add to the size of the estates held by a few individuals —a state of things which Liberals have always been the first to deplore.

It will be worth while quoting a few lines from a speech on this measure made in the Cortes by a very famous man of letters, the Duke of Rivas. Here was no blind reactionary, but a man of culture and progressive ideas, who during Ferdinand's reign had gone into exile with the Liberals, had lived in England and France and was an intimate friend of John Hookham Frere.[2] And Rivas could find no words strong enough to condemn the confiscation of the property of the Orders. It was "barbarous, atrocious, cruel, anti-economical and anti-political." "We all know," he said, "that the greater part of this property had been given to the Orders by the religious themselves; it represented their own capital. Is it not robbery to have taken this from them? . . . And what has been the result of it all? A dozen or so speculators who live on the people's misery have become wealthy. . . . Colossal fortunes—a bitter contrast with the misery in the provinces—have sprung up in no time. The

[1] The buildings of the old University of Alcalá de Henares, for example, fetched 15,000 pesetas (£600 at par); an estate of 5,500 acres containing 20,000 trees went for £560; and various buildings were sold at a few shillings, or a pound or two, apiece. Of the 2,120 religious houses seized, only 685 found purchasers, and the total sum received for them (£210,000 at par) was £10,000 less than the cost of the new House of Congress, which had just been erected—ironically enough—on the site of the demolished Convent of the Holy Spirit (Antequera, *La Desamortización*, etc., pp. 226–7).

[2] Cf. E. Allison Peers: *Rivas and Romanticism in Spain* (Liverpool, 1923) and *Angel de Saavedra, Duque de Rivas, a Critical Study* (New York, Paris, 1923).

religious houses have disappeared, their property has been squandered away, jewels and treasures have been stolen—and has the lot of our people been improved in even the slightest degree? No: the religious houses have gone and what have we to show for them? Rubbish-heaps—mud—depression—tears."[1]

To those who, whatever their political opinions, believe in justice and fair play, it is some consolation that Mendizábal's spoliation brought him a rapid diminution of prestige. "Nothing had come of all his vast schemes and promises, the deficit in the budget was greater, the national credit was lower than ever."[2] Government stock, which had fallen rapidly from 80 to 26, remained at this low level or fell even lower. Mendizábal had made an enemy of the Queen Regent; for, though so many of the clergy supported Don Carlos, she was still loyal to the Church. Naturally, the "progressive" reaction, worn out by its own violence, soon spent itself; Mendizábal fell, and, only two months after playing his trump card, was forced to give place to his "Moderate" adversary, Istúriz. Years afterwards, a statue of him was erected in Madrid, the site chosen for it being very appropriately the site of the Mercedarian monastery in the Plaza del Progreso which had suffered so greatly in the 1834 riots.

The "Moderate" reaction was also short, and, after a new and comparatively Liberal Constitution had been passed (April 27, 1837), binding itself, among much else, "to maintain the worship and the ministers of the Catholic religion professed by Spaniards," a fresh attempt was made to promote legislation penalizing the Church very little less than that of Mendizábal. With the exception of the Escolapians—allowed to remain in their civil character as a teaching Order—the Hospitaller Orders and certain communities of Sisters of Mercy, the religious Orders were

---

[1] *Heterodoxos*, VII, 257.   [2] Butler Clarke, *op. cit.*, p. 120.

suppressed all over the country. Nor was any more religious nonsense talked about the desires of founders or the honour of Divine worship. Such property of the Orders as had not already been disposed of was to be sold forthwith and the proceeds were to be made over to the Caja de Amortización and applied to the extinction of the Public Debt. The fact that the new Constitution had imposed upon the State the responsibility for maintaining Divine worship provided a pretext for the abolition of tithes and first-fruits (July 29, 1837) and for the confiscation of the property of the secular clergy, which was declared national property, whether acquired by gift, by purchase or by any other means whatsoever.

At last the persecutors of the Church had come out into the open. Long ago, the reasons for their actions had been at least plausible; later, these actions might seem to the unprejudiced observer slightly suspect; now it was clear that the attacks were being largely prompted by enmity. The Orders having been, as was thought, extinguished, steps were now taken against the Church as a whole. "The Church is like an old building," remarked a prominent man of the day; "we must pull it right down."[1] Needless to say, it was not buildings that were in his mind, but things more fundamental. So ordinations were forbidden, and sees which became vacant were not filled. Nor were natural causes responsible for the vacancies. The Archbishop of Saragossa and the Bishops of Urgel and León were exiled; the Archbishop of Tarragona, finding his life threatened, escaped on an English boat to Italy; the Archbishops of Seville and Jaén and the Bishops of Pamplona, Orihuela, Plasencia and Mondoñedo were "withdrawn" from their dioceses and imprisoned. Eighteen bishoprics and one hundred and twenty collegiate churches were suppressed in these years. And the state of affairs was worse in practice

[1] *Heterodoxos*, VII, 250.

than in theory. By 1837 more than half the dioceses in the country were without their chief pastors. Six years later the proportion was still much the same. Of the sixty-two sees, thirty-two were vacant; and of the thirty Bishops nominally in possession of their sees, six were imprisoned and nine exiled.[1]

Notwithstanding the continued spoliations, the country became poorer than ever. Much of the confiscated property remained unsold; some of it, as we have seen, had fetched the poorest prices; the Carlist War dragged on; and no Heaven-sent genius arose to save the financial situation. Not only the land of the Church, but the very treasure from the Cathedrals, had been seized to pay for the victory over Carlism which came only in 1839. In the following January a newly elected Moderate Government attempted to render the Church belated justice by stemming the steady process of secularization, but under the regency of Espartero (1840–3) reaction got to work once more. No more money was to be made out of the Orders, whose property had long ago been disposed of, but the sale of the possessions of the secular clergy was resumed with all possible speed. Even Church plate was freely auctioned and altars were stripped of their finely carved and gilded reredoses to bring in more money. Against all this the Vatican's vicegerent, or *chargé d'affaires*, in Madrid protested, with the result that he was expelled from the country as the Nuncio had been earlier, and all relations with Rome were broken. The Pope now delivered a stern allocution recapitulating the attacks on the Church made by successive Liberal Governments. Things had in fact come to such a pass that under any Liberal Government the Church was at the mercy of the plunderer.[2]

[1] Antequera: *La Desamortización*, etc., p. 222; *Heterodoxos*, VII, 239–63.
[2] A. A. Parker (*The Catholic Church in Spain*, pp. 15–16) summarizes further events of these years. His pamphlet should be read with this and the next chapter, as being concerned with the Church as a whole rather than with the Orders.

In 1843, with the opening of the period of majority rule of Ferdinand's daughter Isabel, which came to an end with her deposition a quarter of a century later, began what is known as the "moderate decade." The stern measures against the Church were now mitigated. Parish priests and dignitaries who had been exiled or imprisoned were reinstated. New Bishops were consecrated (out of over fifty, only ten had been in occupation of their sees two years earlier) and prelates were authorized to fill vacant benefices and to confer Holy Orders. The Cortes voted a new measure (*Ley de Culto y Clero*) for the maintenance of Divine worship, which had been disgracefully neglected; sixteen months later, the sales of the property of the secular clergy were suspended and such of it as had not been disposed of was restored to its owners. How much this amounted to may be imagined from the fact that in Madrid alone forty-four churches or religious houses had been pulled down or converted to profane uses: several had become Government offices; one was a factory; one a barracks; one a riding-school; and so on. It may be added that, in the forty years following, 64 more were to be similarly treated, together with 34 such buildings in Barcelona, 52 in Seville, 41 in Cádiz, 33 in Valencia—650, in short, in a total of 63 cities.

Yet another Constitution, which renounced most of the basic principles of its predecessor, was passed in 1845, but this in itself did the Church little service since even the Liberal Constitutions had paid formal homage to the Catholic religion. Narváez, however, a Liberal of a moderate type, was anxious for a reconciliation with Rome, and in this desire many joined him, for the vast majority of Spaniards were repelled by the attacks which had been made on what they held so dear, and which, aimed though they were at communities once reputed to have been rich, actually hit the poorest in the land. So the politicians cast about for some basis of permanent agreement which should secure to the Church fair treatment in the future. It was not easy to find one, in view of the record of the past decade and the impossibility of restoring to the Church, either in money or in kind, all the property which had been taken from it. A draft Concordat produced in 1845 was unacceptable to the Government. The following year saw the accession of Pius IX, who almost at once opened negotiations for a more stable peace. An Apostolic Delegate, sent to Madrid, made contact with the Government; in 1848, the year of so much turmoil in Europe, a Joint Committee was formed, representing Rome and Madrid; and after labouring for some three years the Committee produced the Concordat of October 17, 1851, the ratification of which by both parties restored normal relations, after a period of fourteen years' suspension, between Spain and the Vatican.

CHAPTER III

THE ORDERS AND THEIR HISTORY FROM
1851 TO 1931

THE CONCORDAT of 1851 grappled seriously with the causes of the long-standing discord between Church and State and at first seemed to give every prospect of permanent harmony. In what is primarily a sketch of the recent history of the religious Orders in Spain, we cannot attempt the lengthy task of describing and discussing the terms of the Concordat as a whole. It must suffice to say that the State at last formally recognized the injustice of the continual confiscations of Church property. To restore the capital value of all that had been taken was clearly impossible: between 1821 and 1849 property belonging to the regulars had been sold valued at £31,416,000 sterling and property of the seculars valued at £7,783,000 sterling.[1] But the State agreed to make such compensation as it could by binding itself thereafter to pay the stipends of the clergy. This was not altogether an innovation: for the last fourteen years the Constitution had made the State responsible for the maintenance of public worship—a fact which had been used as an argument to justify spoliation. But laxity and inequality had characterized the provision made: a petition dated 1845, for example, records that in the province of Jaén twenty-three parish priests had received only one-fifth of their stipends since 1841, while in 1846 a group of priests in the province of Orense reported that for two years they had had no stipends at all. The payments were now to be put on a regular basis, in consideration of which the Vatican was to recognize the legal validity of the sales of expropriated possessions.

[1] Antequera: *La Desamortización*, etc., p. 457.

This arrangement was by no means wholly satisfactory. For one thing, it put the clergy in a position of dependence upon the State, and, as time went on, the reasons for their payment by the State became forgotten and they began to be spoken of, especially by their enemies, as though they were State officials. For another thing, the stipends paid to the parochial clergy were very meagre;[1] at best they have received much less than what for educated people can be called a decent living wage and of late years they have suffered cruelly from the fact that, while the purchasing power of money has steadily diminished, their stipends have not been increased. At the same time, the terms of the Concordat clearly established a fact which might often be forgotten but could no longer be disputed: that the clergy were receiving their meagre salaries from the State not as a *privilege*, but as a *right*—i.e., because their predecessors had been victims of the State's aggression.

No compensation, it will be observed, was offered to the religious Orders for the loss of the property belonging to each Order individually. Yet to them, too, the Concordat was the most important enactment of the century, for hitherto not only had whatever fresh property they might acquire been at the mercy of any predatory Finance Minister, but their very existence in Spain might come to an end if a Government were minded to terminate it. The Concordat enabled them at last to settle down peacefully, and for over eighty years their right to be in Spain, though several times challenged, was never in serious danger.

This matter requires rather more detailed consideration than any previously dealt with, for unsympathetic writers have often accused the Orders of having obtained authority to remain or settle in Spain by a trick. "The law," says a typical commentator, "had been so far relaxed as to permit the re-establishment of the Order of St. Vincent of Paul,

---

[1] Cf. p. 30, above.

St. Philip Neri and one other among those approved by the Holy See. In practice the phrase 'one other' was interpreted by the Bishops, not as one for the whole of Spain, but as one in each diocese; and at the request of the Bishops congregations of all kinds established themselves."[1] The trick, if such it had been, was not very clever, and it might have been supposed that such casuistical experts as anti-clericals represent religious as being could have invented a much more effective one. For obviously there are, and have long been, many more than three Orders in each diocese, and therefore, if the provisions of the Concordat were as is suggested, it was being openly broken almost from the first and the equivocal interpretation was hardly worth inventing. It cannot be supposed that Pius IX would have accepted, still less been party to, an arrangement which would have put the Church in the wrong from the outset.

The truth is that the terms of the Concordat are vague in the extreme and can be interpreted harshly or liberally according to taste. But its vagueness cannot in fairness be blamed exclusively upon the Church, as the manner of some is. When two parties draw up and sign an agreement, each party has a share in the responsibility. The Concordat of 1851 is, in this respect as in others which do not here concern us, a compromise in which, we may be sure, either side obtained as much, and conceded as little, as it could. If the result was not what one of the parties had hoped, the other must not be held to account for it.

The most important article is the twenty-ninth, which reads textually as follows:

> To the end that, throughout the Peninsula, there may be a sufficient number of evangelical workers[2] and ministers who may be used by prelates for conducting missions in the towns of their dioceses, may help their

[1] J. B. Trend: *The Origins of Modern Spain*, Cambridge, 1934, p. 145.
[2] *Operarios*: literally, priests who assist the sick and dying.

parish priests, assist the sick and perform other works of charity and public utility, Her Majesty's Government proposes duly to improve the colleges for overseas missionaries and will therefore make the necessary arrangements for the establishment, wherever needful, after first hearing the views of the diocesan prelates, of religious congregations and houses of St. Vincent of Paul, St. Philip Neri, and another Order from among those approved by the Holy See, which shall serve at the same time as places of retreat for ecclesiastics, for the performance of spiritual exercises and for other pious purposes.

There is the article.[1] It must have seemed unsatisfactory to the Orders themselves, for it lays stress on everything but the primary reason for which they take their vows—self-dedication to the life of prayer. But it must have been even less agreeable to those who wished to destroy the religious life in Spain root and branch, for it not only lays down that three Orders are to remain in the country, but represents Her Majesty's Government as proposing their "establishment, wherever needful" and also as proposing to make the arrangements for it. That is the point to observe. There is no question whatever of "permitting" (the word used by the commentator quoted above) the re-establishment of these three Orders: they are introduced on the initiative of the Government and by the Government's agency.

This is made clearer still in Article 35, which says that

---

[1] Article 30, relating to women's Orders, reads: "To the end that there may likewise be religious houses for women wherein all may follow their vocation who are called to the contemplative life and to the active life of assisting the sick, teaching children (*niñas*) and occupying themselves both with things pious and with things useful to the places where they live, the Institute of the Daughters of Charity shall be retained under the direction of the clergy of St. Vincent of Paul and the Government shall be responsible for its support. Likewise shall be retained the religious houses which combine with the contemplative life the education and instruction of children (*niñas*) or other works of charity. With respect to the remaining Orders, the ordinary (*prelados ordinarios*), having regard to all the circumstances of their respective dioceses, shall decide (*propondrán*) in what houses of nuns it is fitting that novices shall be admitted and professed and what exercises of teaching and charity it is convenient to establish in them."

"Her Majesty's Government will provide the means necessary to the subsistence of the religious congregations and houses referred to in Article 29"; while Article 13 of the 1860 Convenio[1] ratifies "what is laid down in the Concordat . . . with regard to the maintenance of the religious congregations and houses established in the Peninsula." From this it follows that the three Orders were to be, not simply tolerated, but maintained by the State, and in fact Royal Decrees of July 23 and December 3, 1852, did make provision for the establishment, in Madrid and other cities, of the congregations of St. Vincent of Paul and St. Philip Neri.

Nothing whatever is expressly laid down regarding all the remaining Orders, and the interpretation put upon this silence by the Church was that these Orders could establish houses in Spain if they wished, but at their own expense—not at that of the Government. In support of this interpretation there is Article 1, which plainly and incontrovertibly says that the Catholic, Apostolic and Roman religion shall be retained in Spain, *"with all the rights and prerogatives which it should enjoy according to the law of God and the dispositions of the Sacred Canons"*; Article 4, which lays it down that "in all other things pertaining to the right and exercise of the ecclesiastical authority and to the ministry of Sacred Orders, the Bishops and the clergy dependent on them shall enjoy the full liberty established by the Sacred Canons"; and, above all, Article 43, according to which "all else pertaining to ecclesiastical things or persons concerning which no provision is made in the foregoing articles shall be directed and administered according to the canonically ruling discipline of the Church."

There seems, then, no reason to find fault with the interpretation set upon these articles by the Church. If the State objected, it had only to say so; but it is a matter of history, which can be verified from State correspondence and

[1] Cf. p. 86, below.

references in the official *Gaceta de Madrid*, that the Governments of the time and the Holy See were in complete agreement on the matter. The arrangement found general favour: the Orders, to the great good of the country, were allowed to remain or return; and from this date their beneficent work, so well known to us to-day, was carried on without hindrance. It may be added that Articles 35 and 41 of the Concordat formally recognize the capacity of the Orders to hold property; though, as will be seen, they have had little enough opportunity to do so.

During the decade which followed the Concordat continual attempts were made to destroy it or limit its application. A revolution in July 1854 was followed by a biennium dubbed "progressive" by those who approved of its works and "luckless" by those who did not. On May 1, 1855, a disentailment measure was passed, in defiance of the Concordat, as radical as any which had preceded it. This *Ley de Desamortización*, as it was termed, expropriated all property remaining to the Orders or newly acquired by them, together with the unsold property returned to the Church under the Concordat, this property to be disposed of in small lots on easy terms of payment so as to attract a new class of buyer. It also made an attack on religious houses for women, suppressing the smaller houses and forbidding the admission of further novices. The Queen refused, as well she might, to sign laws so quickly and cynically breaking a treaty. Eventually, seeing no alternative but abdication and revolution, she yielded under protest to her ministers' demands. Church and people, however, protested as best they could: Bishops formally, for which crime they were sent into exile; lay folk by means of demonstrations, some of which became dangerous and had to be suppressed. The Vatican made the only possible move by at once breaking off diplomatic relations.

But this irresponsible Government met protests with fresh

7   85

excesses. In 1856 expropriation was extended to "all property possessed or being enjoyed by individuals or corporations of an ecclesiastical character": a few exceptions were made but none of these applied to the Orders. In view of the wide measure of general approval which had been given to the recently enacted Concordat it was impossible that measures so flagrantly contravening it should remain for long in force. The latter was almost still-born; the former was immediately repealed on the advent to power of the Narváez-Nocedal Government of October 1856. When the Queen opened the Cortes on May Day, 1857, she was able to claim that this new Government had restored the nation's honour by "re-establishing in all its vigour the Concordat made with the Holy See."

In 1860 a new settlement, known as the Convenio, was made between the State and the Holy See, by which the Government confirmed its recognition of the status of the Church in Spain embodied in the 1851 Concordat and recognized without limitation or reserve the right of the Church to acquire any kind of property. The estates still held by the Church, it was agreed, should be sold and the proceeds invested in 3 per cent stock which should become inalienable Church property. The amount of money obtained was found, as previously, to be very small but the principle was important.[1]

So, it seemed, the Church was left at peace—but not for long. In 1868 came the political revolution which dethroned Isabel II and plunged Spain into seven years of chaos. No sovereign, other than a Bourbon, could be found; after two years, Amadeo, an Italian prince, accepted the throne, but at the end of two more, abdicated; a Republic, which in one year alone had four presidents, proved a hopeless failure; and at the beginning of 1875 a Bourbon returned in the person of Isabel's young son Alfonso.[2]

[1] La Fuente, VI, 400–5.
[2] For a summary of this period, see *Heterodoxos*, VII, 425–50.

Less than a fortnight after the Queen's departure, the passion for despoiling the Church broke out anew. The Revolutionary Junta had at once proclaimed the freedom of the Press, the freedom of associations, freedom of worship, freedom to teach—in all, no less than sixteen varieties of freedom. But it then proceeded to invalidate its own principles by denying this freedom to those with whom it disagreed. Its idea of granting freedom of associations was to suppress all religious communities established since 1837, to dissolve the Society of Jesus in Spain, together with the Order of St. Vincent of Paul, and to confiscate their possessions. Convents it reduced to one-half of their number and no compensation whatever was given to the religious who were driven from their homes. Freedom to teach it interpreted by drastically curtailing the teaching facilities of the religious Orders. This was a strange application of the principles of a revolution which took liberty for its watchword—meaning, of course, "liberty for the revolters." But so it has ever been in Spain. Intolerance on one side has been met by intolerance on the other. Exalting the freedom of the individual, the revolution denied it to the harmless *frailes*. Proclaiming the respect due to property and home, it robbed one class of citizen of both—a class consisting of persons who had dedicated themselves to the service of God. Never was a revolution more utterly self-condemned; never did a revolutionary *régime* more fully deserve what came to it.

In one part of the country after another broke out attacks upon the Church exceeding in violence even those of 1835. In Madrid, three of the oldest churches and a Dominican monastery were burned down. In Barcelona, two churches and two monasteries were destroyed; the seminary was confiscated and turned into a secondary school; and the church of Sant Jaume, in the centre of the city, was seized with a view to its demolition and the sale of its valuable site. At Reus, near Tarragona, the Discalced Carmelite nuns

87

were driven from their convent, which was destroyed. At Huesca, in Aragon, the Bishop was expelled, three convents were seized, a parish church was destroyed and another was badly damaged. At Valladolid, a church was converted into a club. In Salamanca and a number of other Castilian cities seminaries were seized. At Palencia, rioters sacked a convent, wrecked the Romanesque cloister of the thirteenth-century monastery of Santa María at Aguilar de Campóo and destroyed part of the eleventh-century Benedictine house of San Zoil, at Carrión de los Condes. But the worst harm was done at Seville. There, in one day, the revolutionary council ordered the demolition of no less than fifty-seven churches; while mobs anticipated the fulfilment of the order by destroying two monasteries, together with the mediaeval church of San Miguel, and burning or smashing to pieces statues, reredoses and other works of art without number.

We may well enquire into the motive lying behind these and other actions. We have traced in these pages three reasons for such crimes and acts of injustice—regalism, in the eighteenth century; the poverty of the country, which was used by Liberal Governments during the first half of the nineteenth century as an excuse for plundering the Church while it had anything left to plunder; and anti-clericalism, partly a political motive and partly provoked by the Church's implacable opposition to her despoilers. But will even the last of these motives—the other two having disappeared—explain the frenzy with which the revolutionaries were inspired during these years of chaos and which in our own day has broken out anew?

It will not. And it is here that the fourth motive enters—a motive which in the sixties was slowly emerging, and which was shortly to gain force with the growth of proletarian movements, the most advanced of which was Anarchism. This motive is nothing less than hatred of God.

It was easy for this to mask itself as hatred of the Catholic Church, since the Catholic Church was (and, despite much encouragement recently given to Protestants, still is) almost the sole organization representative of religious institutionalism in the country. But there are clear signs that the revolutionaries were now attacking not so much the Church as its Founder.

The politicians gave the country a lead. Among the members of parliament who spoke in the debates of 1869, on the new Constitution, were many who quite openly declared their rejection of Christianity. Said Roberto Robert: "I have never believed in the Divinity or in any mystery. I have no religious feelings." Said Díaz Quintero: "The Catholic religion, like all other religions, is false. . . . I will have no relation with God, not even for the purpose of denying him." Fernando Garrido asserted that the recent revolution had been "an anti-religious revolution, rather than a political one." "God is but a product of reason," exclaimed Pi y Margall, one of the heroes of the First Republic, "and Catholicism is dead in the conscience of humanity and in the conscience of the Spanish people."

There was much more of the kind in these debates: one day's session became generally known as the "Session of Blasphemies." But the spirit animating these unfortunately named Liberals may most suitably be expressed in the words of Suñer y Capdevila: "Faith, Heaven, God are decrepit ideas; the new ideas are science, earth, man. . . . I could wish the Spaniards had no religion and I hope to devote myself fully to the propagation of this splendid doctrine." "*¡Guerra a Dios!*" was his concluding cry. "War upon God!"[1]

The cry was a faint one, but it was soon to be taken up with increasing volume. Within a decade, the European proletarian movement which recognized Marx as its leader

[1] *Heterodoxos*, VII, 430–1.

had split, through the quarrel of Marx with Bakunin. There had emerged the Anarchists, whose decentralizing and destructive political ideals have made such a strong appeal in individualistic Spain. It is in this way that Spain has gradually become a nursery for their atheistic doctrines, to which we shall return later.

The Constitution of 1869, when passed, was found again to be paying lip-service to freedom, for its seventeenth article assured to all Spaniards the free right of association provided public morals were not harmed thereby. But it was short-lived. Throughout Amadeo's reign of two years and a quarter, the Church continued to suffer. In one part of the country after another, religious houses were closed or confiscated by the Government; an attempt was made to suppress the use of the word "God" in official documents and another to release the State from its obligations to the parish clergy under the Concordat. With the coming of the First Republic, in February 1873, the mobs got to work again, especially in the South. At Málaga, on March 6, 1873, the Mercedarian and Capuchin friaries were destroyed. At Cádiz, where schools were deprived of the names of their patron saints and re-dedicated to such patrons as "Reason" and "Equality," the city council turned a community of nuns out of their convent and would have pulled it down had not mobs anticipated them, choosing Good Friday for the work of destruction. Religious statues which had remained undamaged were removed from public places; portraits of clergy and religious were taken from picture-galleries; a Franciscan friary and church were turned by the munici-pality into a "Federal Club for Workers"; other churches were pulled down and one was confiscated for conversion into a fish-market.

In the centre and north, similar events took place, though with less frequency. At Palencia, in one day of rioting—May 2, 1874—the churches of the city were invaded and profaned; statues were smashed, books were torn up, furniture was destroyed and the Host was trampled underfoot. In Barcelona, too, mobs profaned the churches and the authorities forbade Divine worship and even the private administration of the viaticum. As far away as Galicia there were riots. In the little town of Bande, near Orense, sixty men were killed for having attempted to prevent the plundering of their churches. Semi-official attacks on the Church also continued. The stipends of the clergy were again allowed to fall into arrears. From this and that part of Spain the teaching Orders were driven by violence; seminaries and religious schools were confiscated, and the more radical groups, as they continually pressed for power, pressed also for means to restrict the Orders' influence. It was not surprising that Carlism again gathered strength and that the Second Carlist War, which lasted until 1876, seemed less and less a dynastic struggle and more and more a religious crusade. "God, country and king!" was the threefold Carlist motto—and God came first. It was a clear reply to the challenge: "War upon God!"

When Alfonso XII came to the throne, he was able to appeal successfully to the religious zeal of the Carlists and lost no time in ending the War. "If you are fighting for the Catholic faith," he assured them, "I am a Catholic King and will right the wrong done to the Church." He kept his promise. Freedom of association was again guaranteed by Article 13 of the 1876 Constitution, under which Spain was continuously governed until 1923. The 1851 Concordat once more, with but few modifications, came into force. The clergy received the arrears of stipend which many of them so sorely needed. At the same time, Article 11 allowed freedom of worship to others than Catholics, though it forbade "public manifestations" of other forms of religion. This, though not fully acceptable to those who advocate complete freedom of worship, was perhaps as much as could then be expected in a country where for so long and until so recent a date the Church had been singled out for persecution. The seeds of tolerance, thus sown, grew apace, and as the years went on the article was interpreted with increasing liberality.

For a period of over half a century, the Orders, and, with occasional lapses, the Church as a whole, were now allowed the toleration for which they had hoped in 1851. Various attempts, however, were made to take away the Church's freedom. Article 13 of the 1876 Constitution called for some amplification, which it received in the "Law of Associations" passed in 1887. The somewhat vaguely worded second article of this Act exempted from its provisions the congregations established by the State under the 1851 Concordat but required all others to submit to it. Now between 1876 and the end of the century a number of fresh Orders and Congregations were established in Spain—among them some which have proved most beneficent in public service. All these, of course, received canonical approval, but the superiors of about sixty of them, who had profited by reading their history, took the precaution of obtaining the sanction of the secular authorities, not because this was necessary but as a defence against possible attacks on the part of hostile Governments in the future.

They were well advised. At the beginning of the twentieth century, a "progressive" Home Secretary, Alfonso González, revived the fiction of the illegality of all the Orders but three. Had his contention been correct, he would have been acting logically in pressing for the expulsion of the remainder. All he demanded, however (under a Royal Order dated September 19, 1901), was that the remaining Orders should, within six months, register under the Law of Associations and observe its provisions. But it was late in the day, after exactly fifty years, to attempt to re-define the Concordat. On the one hand, the Holy See and the Spanish hierarchy protested that the Royal Order was an infringement of it; on the other, a great popular movement began in defence of the Orders, which, having been given a few years' peace to pursue their work, had established themselves as never before in the popular affection. Within a few months, a compromise—or *modus vivendi* as it was called—was effected: the communities which had already obtained a State licence were exempted from registration; others were required to submit to registration as a pure formality, on fulfilment of which condition they would be exempted from further compliance with the law's provisions.

This by no means ended the negotiations. The *modus vivendi* was legalized by a Royal Order, and in 1904 an attempt was made to effect a permanent solution to the problem by the drafting of a new Convenio to define more fully the position of bodies which had fulfilled the conditions of this Order. These were to be exempted from the Law of Associations and placed under Canon Law provided they observed the laws of the country, but on the other hand they were to receive no kind of subsidy or other aid from State funds and were to pay taxes on property and income like any other bodies. No new Orders were to be allowed, except after agreement between the Government of the day and the Holy See, and no new houses were to be established without the joint authorization of the Diocesan Bishop and a Royal Order. With certain exceptions religious houses having fewer than twelve inmates were to be suppressed and all religious houses were required to register with a special department of the Ministry of Worship and Justice. These regulations were to apply only to Orders and Congregations: all other bodies of a religious nature would be brought under the Law of Associations.

The Convenio, which was a reasonably fair one, passed the Senate after the summer recess, but before it could reach the stage of discussion by the Lower House the

Ministry fell, and in the end it shared a fate which has befallen many other measures, good and bad, under the Spanish parliamentary system. In 1906, the Home Secretary in the Liberal López Domínguez Government presented in its place a new Law of Associations on the lines of González' decree. This not only evoked a united protest from the episcopate but was so unpopular that it divided even the Liberals. It, too, failed to pass the Cortes; the best solution that could eventually be found was a new compromise—a Royal Order, issued in 1910, which did little more than confirm that of 1902.

At the end of 1910 was passed the famous "Padlock Law" (*Ley del Candado*) which arose from circumstances created by the expulsion of religious Orders from France and the apprehension that Spain might suffer an invasion on a large scale from abroad. This law provided that no new associations belonging to Orders or Congregations already recognized in Spain should be allowed for two years without a special authorization from the Ministry of Worship and Justice, such authorization not to be given if more than one-third of the members of the proposed group were foreigners. The Holy See naturally protested; the Spanish Ambassador left the Vatican; demonstrations on both sides became frequent. But the law was not without its defenders among Spanish Catholics, especially after the Portuguese Revolution of October 1910 had sent the King into exile, established a Republic and driven numerous monks and nuns to seek refuge abroad. A paragraph added to the Law by way of amendment during its passage through the Senate provided that, should no new Law of Associations be passed within two years, this Law should automatically cease to have effect. In both Houses, the debate was largely between extremists; one writer described it as a tussle in the eighteenth-century style between a new type of regalist and a new type of ultramontane. The Bill was soon approved by the Senate, but Congress debated it with great heat, before passing it, in a small House, by 174 votes to 54. Though there were obvious objections to the Law, it went some way towards assuring what, if my own experience is reliable, most Spaniards desire—that the large majority of monks and nuns in Spain shall be Spanish. To that extent it was not generally unpopular.

In 1911, an unsuccessful attempt by Canalejas to introduce a new and severe Law of Associations brought the religious troubles of Alfonso XIII's reign to an end. From 1912, when diplomatic relations with the Vatican were restored, till 1931, when they were once more imperilled, there were no serious political differences or social upheavals related with ecclesiastical questions. The position of the religious Orders was now clearly defined; of their property there was no more left to confiscate; and anti-clericalism, though to some it might appear to be growing, was probably at most stationary. The reason for its apparent growth was the fact that it was being fomented and exploited to the utmost by men whose destructive desires went deeper, and who, to adapt a recent metaphor of one of their own publicists, used the anti-clerical mask to hide the anti-God face.

These were the Anarchists—or Anarcho-Syndicalists, as they called themselves for political purposes, uniting with the Syndicalist Unions but retaining also their own organization to ensure the preservation and transmission of their doctrines in all their purity. They had gained a footing in Spain before the death of their prophet and leader, Michael Bakunin.[1] Politically, they aim at destroying government in the generally understood sense of that word and substituting for it a state of harmony which they believe would come into being between the free groups which they would create to take its place. Their creed consists in a series of denials,

[1] See E. H. Carr: *Michael Bakunin* (London, 1937) and E. Allison Peers: "Bakunin and Spanish Anarchism," in *Studies* (Dublin, March 1938), pp. 136–41.

and, though these include institutions as generally considered essential as the State, the country, government,
marriage, family life and individual property, the important
point for our purpose is that first on the list comes God.
"If there were no God," Voltaire once said, "it would be
necessary to invent him." "If there were a God," exclaims
Juan Peiró, a contemporary Anarchist, "it would be both
human and natural to destroy him."[1] That Spanish
Anarchists of to-day teach atheism to their children we may
learn from the *Cartilla Filológica*, a child's reading-book
which denies the existence of God and the soul's immor-
tality. They parody the Nicene Creed: "I believe in
Revolutionary Socialism Almighty, son of Justice and
Anarchy," and so on—the parody in its entirety is too painful
to Christian feeling to be reproduced.

Atheism, then, stands at the head of the Anarchists'
beliefs, and, as their movement has been extending and
growing, with short exceptional periods of arrest and decline,
for over sixty years, the fact of its having affected the religious
situation is not surprising. Throughout this period of peace
between Church and State the Anarchists indulged in
displays of what they called "direct action"[2]—riots, strikes,
incendiary outbursts and assassinations—in which churches,
monasteries, convents and seminaries often suffered and of
which the worst example was the "Tragic Week" of 1909.
The centre of this demonstration was Barcelona, in which
city alone sixty-three of such buildings were burned and
one hundred and fifty persons were killed, chiefly priests and
religious. In nearly all the towns within easy reach of
Barcelona, similar events took place, and the desecration of

[1] For the exact terminology and context of this remark, see my *Catalonia
Infelix*, p. 292.
[2] As the French Anarchist song has it:
> Nos pères jadis ont dansé
> au son du canon du passé!
> Maintenant la danse tragique
> demande plus forte musique.
> (*Refrain*) Dynamitons, dynamitons.

cemeteries and the profanation of dead bodies added a new feature of horror to the tragedy.

For most, if not all, of the riots described in the foregoing pages it has been possible to find a rational cause either in the behaviour or attitude of the clergy or in misconceptions entertained about them. But these were different. The clergy had nothing to do with them. They arose out of a revolutionary strike declared by the Anarcho-Syndicalists in defiance of one of the institutions which they "denied"— the State. And in the course of the strike they took the opportunity of defying another of the institutions which they "denied"—God. True, they attacked religion under a certain form—the only form in which they had experience of it—but if Spain had been a Protestant country they would have attacked it none the less. How could they do otherwise, holding such principles and believing, with Marx, that religion is the opium of the people and that belief in God "brutifies man and makes him docile, slavish and resigned to every kind of insult and debasement"?[1] It was a case, as Josep Carner—no clerical—once said, of "cold fanaticism." This is absolutely fundamental to an understanding of the situation in Spain to-day. To minimize its importance is to play into the hands of anti-Christ. To deny it is to refuse to accept facts.

[1] Gil Maestre, p. 113. Cf. Carreras, pp. 14–16.

CHAPTER IV

THE ORDERS AND THE SPANISH PEOPLE

BEFORE CONSIDERING the later history of the religious Orders in Spain it may be well to try to form some idea of what they do for the people. Those who attack the *frailes*—seldom, as we have said, from first-hand knowledge— are accustomed to represent them either as unfortunate beings immured against their will in the cloister and condemned to spend their lives in unnatural confinement or as social parasites content to live in comfortable idleness at the expense of their communities, which in their turn are subsidized by misguided benefactors. To all instructed persons the ludicrousness of this caricature is evident. Many religious bring to their Orders property, the income of which would more than suffice to keep them—and for communal sharing among Christians there is the best and earliest Biblical authority. Further, the Orders spend their incomes, as quickly as they get them, in feeding, clothing and educating the poor, and many religious who in the world could easily maintain themselves in comfort work more strenuously than they ever did in the world for the privilege of living in conditions of Spartan poverty. I think, for example, of a Benedictine community, well known to me, existing on food which an English Benedictine found it difficult to eat at all; or of a Dominican scholar of world-wide fame working for long hours in his cell through the bitter Castilian winter with his lower limbs wrapped for warmth in a blanket.

So much for "comfort." The charge of idleness can best be met by an enquiry into the occupations of some of the representative Orders, other than their primary occupation—

that strenuous and many-sided exercise which for brevity we call "prayer." On this last it is unnecessary to enlarge, for while those with experience of prayer will need no convincing, to those without it the very phrase just used will be meaningless. But everyone can understand when it is said that the Orders are in closest touch with the people and spend themselves in their service. And of the truth of this a very brief experience of monastery life will convince one. Quite apart from the more ambitious social and educational activities shortly to be described, the constant ministrations of the Orders to the poor are of incalculable value in a country which has many unemployed and no dole for them.

In October 1931, when the proposal to expel the religious Orders from Spain was before the Cortes, I wrote an article[1] which was widely quoted both at the time and later, testifying to the affection with which the Orders were regarded by the people. At that time, before agitations inspired by the left-wing extremists were in full swing, there was but little feeling against them, nor for that matter does it appear since to have developed proportionately with the feeling against the Church and religion in general. I pointed out in 1931 how such impressions generally come from contaminated sources. Some years previously, an English resident in a large Spanish city had given me most vivid and detailed illustrations of "how the people hate the priests." Soon afterwards, I discovered that my informant knew but a few words of Spanish and had drawn his impressions from a single Spaniard—a politician who spoke English fluently but who soon afterwards became notorious as one of the fiercest enemies of Catholicism in the country.[2]

[1] *Church Times*, October 17, 1931.
[2] Another interesting illustration of the unreliability of personal impressions unsupported by knowledge appears as this book goes to press. Mr. George Orwell, who spent some time in Spain during the early months of the War, and whose *Homage to Catalonia*, though defective as regards Spanish history and politics, shows a genuine desire to be fair to the side which does not enjoy

No doubt there were, and are, many persons in Spain who dislike and distrust the Orders, but probably no more than dislike and distrust the Civil Guard, the Catalonians or the League of Nations. At any rate, if they are distrusted, it is certainly not by the poor, the sick or the hungry. How often have I stood outside the Carthusian Monastery of Miraflores and watched the long trail of poor folk coming slowly up the steep hill from Burgos to receive their allowance of food from the hands of the Prior! And such scenes are, of course, commonplaces all over the country.

That their goodness to well-to-do and needy alike is met by the respect and affection of a large majority of those whom they serve is beyond question. Cultured and intelligent people send their children to the schools of the religious Orders rather than to State schools because they know that by so doing they can rely upon their receiving a good education: the irreligious may decry these schools as much as they please but too many of Spain's leading intellectuals and statesmen have been educated in them for such attacks to have much effect. Again, it is remarkable how many earnest and thinking young people attend the churches of the religious Orders rather than the parish churches, and choose monks for their confessors and directors rather than the secular clergy.

Of the friendliness to the Orders of the poorer classes scores of illustrations could be given. I remember very vividly, some years ago, walking through the city of Ávila

his sympathies, tells us that he was impressed, "in Catalonia and Aragon, in the first year of war," by the "apparent absence of any religious feeling whatever among the mass of the people" (*New English Weekly*, November 24, 1938). Now all who know Catalonia are well aware that that region is second only to the Basque Country—if that—in religious zeal, and that, as I have shown in *Catalonia Infelix*, there was no hostility manifested to the Church there during the Republic as there was in other parts of Spain. Further, countless narratives have described how Catholic worship, proscribed by authority, went on in Catalonian homes and what incredible risks were taken by Catholics who put their religion before everything else. "Admittedly," remarks Mr. Orwell, "it might have been dangerous to admit openly to religious belief—still, one cannot be altogether deceived about a thing like that." He is wrong: one can.

another on historical manuscripts prepared by P. Miguélez. When I was last there, an extensive work on the large collection of Arabic manuscripts was nearly completed and a catalogue of the Hebrew manuscripts was being made. A work on the coin-collection has already appeared; a catalogue of the six thousand prints in the library began to appear some years ago in the Augustinian review, *La Ciudad de Dios*; P. Zarco is also publishing a critical account of the miniatures and other paintings, which form a particularly fine collection.

This is only one aspect of the activities of the Escorial. To it must be added the heavy routine work of the Library, and the personal attention which any serious student may obtain from scholars competent to advise him. It may be imagined what the cost to the State would be to maintain a service of the same efficiency were the State even willing to undertake it. As it is, it costs the State nothing, for the monks work for love.

Besides labouring for the good of students and scholars who visit the Library or consult them by letter, most of the librarians themselves conduct practical investigations. The late P. Miguélez' work on Jansenism; P. Melchor's numerous studies of the history of the Arabs in Spain; P. Nemesio Morata's edition of the Murcian writer Mohidin; P. López Órtiz's work on mediaeval law; and P. Arturo García's edition of the *Castigos y documentos* of Sancho el Bravo are a few examples.

An excellent library too little known by students, and among Augustinian libraries second only to that of El Escorial, is the so-called "Biblioteca de Filipinas," housed in the Colegio de Agustinos Filipinos at Valladolid. This contains, not only books, but also many objects of all kinds, comprising a veritable museum of Philippine life and customs. Its large observatory, sixty years old, was until recently the only one in the province. The library itself is largely devoted to books on the Philippines and other regions in the East where the Augustinians have missions. But there is also an immense collection of theological works, especially of the sixteenth century, when so many Augustinian mystics and ascetics, such as Luis de León, Cristóbal de Fonseca and Pedro Malón de Chaide, were also stylists of high merit. I remember first going to this library for a few hours and finding so much of interest there that I stayed for days.

One could write at great length of the benefits which individual Augustinians have conferred upon scholarship, but it would be wearisome to cite names and writings of theologians, antiquarians, Arabists, Hellenists, Hebraists, philosophers, sociologists, economists, astronomers, naturalists, and so on. Let us rather look at the work done by Augustinians in the lower grades of education, so necessary in modern Spain.

At the Escorial, the College of Higher Studies, since its foundation in 1893, has educated a great many public men—politicians, authors and scientists as well as clergy and religious. Like the other schools on the foundation, it is well equipped with laboratories and workshops, and, like all colleges of the kind, it awards scholarships to its pupils and sets apart an ample number of free places.

In Madrid, the educational work of the Augustinians is comprised by a secondary boarding-school, with three hundred children, most of them poor, a number of night schools for the working-classes, and thirty-three workshops, where clothes are made for poor families and in some of which instruction is given in this work to the daughters of the workmen employed in them. There are also over twenty such workshops in other parts of Spain. Most of the remaining schools of the Augustinians are in the north and centre of Spain. León has a large secondary school, which, when the Republic came, was the only one in the city. Llanes, in Asturias, has another, and there are (or were) free schools of a popular kind at Santander, Portugalete and Trujillo. Bilbao has a large night school open to workers without fee. There are also a number of schools, notably at Uclés, Leganés, Guernica and Valencia de San Juan, for poor boys hoping to be ordained.

Something should be added of the periodical publications of the Augustinians in Spain, which are by no means confined to the field of theology. Every student of Spanish literature, for example, is familiar with the late P. Blanco García's three-volume history of nineteenth-century literature, which in more than a generation has not been superseded. Comparatively few of those who use this work know that its author was a religious, and still fewer have any idea that parts of it, in their original form, appeared as articles in an Augustinian learned review. *La Ciudad de Dios* ("The City of God") was founded as long ago as 1881 by P. Cámara, once a professor at Valladolid and later Bishop of Salamanca. To it was added another, *España y América*; while a third, *El Archivo Histórico-Hispanoamericano*, contained chiefly documents and other source-material for the history of Spain and Spanish America. These three reviews were later combined into one, a monthly entitled *Religión y Cultura*, which appealed to a wider public and published a particularly striking volume ten years ago, on the occasion of the tercentenary celebrations of Fray Luis de León.

Silos, to the few travellers who have visited it, is one of the unforgettable things in Spain. Santo Domingo de Silos, to give it its full title, is a Benedictine monastery situated nearly forty miles south-east of Burgos, on the main Soria road; its comparative isolation brings it fewer visitors than are to be found at the great Charterhouse of Miraflores or at the Cistercian Convent of Las Huelgas, which are only a short walk from the same city. Tourists who penetrate as far as Silos admire the Romanesque doorway which belonged to the original church (the present one is only two hundred years old) and above everything else the magnificent two-storied cloister, of which the lower and the upper story date respectively from the eleventh and the twelfth century. Few of such visitors, even of those who share the hospitality of the monks, realize that they are in a hive of intellectual life and that the very hands which serve them at table may be those of a scholar whose works are known the world over.

The achievements of the Benedictines of Silos fall into two classes: first, they have restored their own monastery with a care and a completeness which the guardians of many a State-owned National Monument might envy; secondly, they have made it one of the best-known centres of scholarship in northern Castile.

In 1880, when, after an absence of forty-five years, the Benedictines returned to Silos, they found it little more than a ruin. The cloister was falling down; grass and weeds grew in what is now the refectory; cows pastured in what was to become a library of thirty thousand volumes; the roofs of the buildings were dilapidated and decayed. Go to Arlanza and Cardeña, in the same province of Burgos, both historic churches and both in ruins. Better still, go to Poblet, near Tarragona, one of the greatest Cistercian houses in mediaeval Spain, which was attacked and burned by fanatical mobs in 1835, and has since been allowed by successive Governments to turn to ruin and decay in the guise of a National Monument. Then go to Silos and see a perfectly restored monastery—not merely restored in body, that is to say, but re-endowed with a soul.

One of the first achievements of the Silos Benedictines was to form a school of palaeography—a study which has been very much neglected in the universities and secular institutions of Spain. The next step was the foundation of an Historical and Archaeological Institute, for which there were abundant opportunities in the immediate locality:

it may be doubted if any region in Spain is better documented than this. One of the French Benedictines who formed part of the original colony wrote two works on Silos itself which were published at the expense of the French Government, besides a number of works on liturgiology, which has long been an outstanding feature of the scholarship of the monastery. P. Casiano Rojo, who died in 1931, specialized in Gregorian music, on which he was one of the foremost Spanish authorities. The Abbot, P. Serrano, has also written on this subject, and his vast industry and encyclopaedic range have produced historical works on Cardeña, Covarrubias (between Silos and Burgos, with a fine Collegiate Church), Arlanza and San Salvador del Moral, four volumes on the diplomatic correspondence between Spain and the Holy See during the Pontificate of Pius V, and a large number of other historical works too numerous to mention. P. Serrano is, as every specialist in Hispanic studies knows, one of the greatest living authorities in his own field and he has been responsible for inspiring much work as well as for producing it: the Silos source-books for the history of Castile, for example, are among the most important of their kind. For want of space, I have omitted all reference to the exclusively Benedictine studies on which the Silos Fathers are continuously engaged, and even with that addition the half would not have been told. Against the petulant and short-sighted policy of those Republicans who in 1931 would have expelled the Orders from Spain, and against the violence and fury of those neo-Republicans who would now gladly do the same, the scholarship as well as the beauty of Silos stands out, with the dignity and the serenity of its labour, an immovable and eternal witness.

In the extreme north-east of Spain is the Benedictine monastery of Montserrat, situated high above the Llobregat valley, thirty miles from Barcelona, in a kind of eyry which

Nature certainly meant to be accessible only with difficulty but which civilization has brought within reach of the million. By road, mountain-railway or air, probably a hundred people visit Montserrat for every one who visits Silos. They remark upon the picturesqueness of the situation, hear the legend of the *Moreneta*, or Black Virgin, and the history of the foundation of the monastery, visit the *Moreneta* in her shrine, listen to the justly famous choir, and go away without having the slightest idea that here, as at Silos, is one of the most notable centres of intellectual activity in the country.

Pride of place in any account of the educational work of Montserrat must be given to its venerable printing-press, founded in 1499—very soon after printing had been introduced into Spain—by its devout and erudite Abbot, García de Cisneros. While the great pride of this institution is its monumental edition of the Bible, which, when completed, will consist of twenty-two volumes of text and ten of illustrations, it has produced works of all kinds, from *éditions de luxe* to small popular books of devotion. Typical of its combination of critical skill with beauty of format is its recently published *Sixteenth-century Bibliography of the Monks of Montserrat*, the compilation of Dom Anselm M. Albareda, who was transferred to Rome shortly before the outbreak of the Civil War.

The library at Montserrat, when I was last there, some five years ago, had 130,000 books, but it has been growing so rapidly that it was probably a great deal larger at the outbreak of the Civil War. We may believe that, when the present troubles are over, it will begin to grow once more. There is also a large music library, for, like so many Benedictine houses, Montserrat has specialized in music, and the Escolanía, a foundation of great antiquity, is one of the famous choir-schools of Europe.

As in the Escorial, so at Montserrat, the outstanding

impression which the library leaves upon one who has suffered from the inadequacy of Spanish State and Provincial libraries is that of efficiency. It is perhaps worth while to insist upon a point, such as this, on which one can speak from long experience. Of the Museums of Montserrat I can only write more generally. The "Biblical Museum" is the creation of P. Ubach, editor-in-chief of the Montserrat Bible. Closely related to it is the Egyptian Museum, planned as a complementary exhibition with the same object of illustrating the Biblical narrative. A third Museum is devoted chiefly to a study of the Montserrat district in all its aspects: the structure and formation of the mountain-range, with its fantastic finger-shaped peaks; the minerals of the region; its animal life, especially its birds and insects; and the flora, not only of the immediate neighbourhood, but of the whole of Catalonia.

When one comes to the individuals who have enriched scholarship by their writings, it is easy to forget how much of the work that they do receives little or no recognition in print. In 1936, for example, a small army of monks was at work upon the cataloguing and arrangement of the ever-growing library, or upon the acquisition of books and manuscripts, in search of which they go all over Europe. Again, it is difficult to estimate the amount of subsidiary labour which has been involved in the production of the Montserrat Bible: some few years ago it came as a surprise to hear that P. Ubiols, who died in the Near East, had been engaged in retracing the whole of the missionary journeys of St. Paul as a contribution to the volumes of the Pauline Epistles. Once more, it is hard to estimate the amount of labour that goes into the huge annual *Analecta Montserratensia*; while thirty monks are normally engaged, wholly or partly, in teaching. It is therefore, perhaps, invidious to mention individual scholars, because their names happen to be more prominently before the intellectual public than those of others. P. Albareda, as I know, always looked upon his unremitting work in the service of the library as of greater importance than his own many publications. P. Ubach would probably speak similarly of the direction of the Montserrat Bible. The learned Abbot, Dom Antonio María Marcet, has spent much unrecorded time in searching for art treasures in various parts of Europe. To these names should be added those of the learned Hellenist, P. Arufat, and P. Suñol, author of various studies on Gregorian Music, who went from Montserrat to Milan, both of whom scholars will always associate with this monastery.

It is difficult to write of such centres of intellectual industry as these merely as such, when so many other aspects of them demand recognition. It must not be supposed that anyone is blind to the beauty and the devotion which radiate in both who has chosen to write primarily of the contributions which they are making to scholarship and education. Nor must it be thought that the Benedictines are not active elsewhere, both within and without Spain. But Silos and Montserrat are such remarkable achievements that they alone would more than justify the continuance of the Order of St. Benedict in Spain, where among the houses of that Order they will always be pre-eminent.

What has been said of the Augustinians and the Benedictines must be taken as representing the type of work done in Spain by the Orders of older foundation. Very reluctantly, for lack of space, I pass over the devoted labours of Dominicans, Franciscans and Carmelites, mentioning only a few of their outstanding scholars. Spain owes much to the Dominican Fathers, especially to their busy hive of industry in Madrid and to that peaceful retreat of San Esteban at Salamanca, of which I can speak from long personal knowledge. Among great Dominican scholars of the past and present, honoured names will always be those of P. Justo

Cuervo, the foremost authority upon Luis de Granada; P. Luis Getino, for so long Chronicler of his Province and founder of *La Ciencia Tomista*; and P. Maximino Llaneza, primarily a theologian and an historian of the Dominican Missions in the East, but also a notable bibliographer, as the four large tomes of his Luis de Granada bibliography testify.

The Franciscans are not primarily erudites, but such theologians and historians as P. Lorenzo Pérez, P. Andrés Ivars and P. Atanasio López have made great reputations outside their Order, and among their publications are two learned reviews which command universal respect. One is the *Archivo Ibero-Americano*—and if any critic doubts the competence of the Franciscans, let him examine the really remarkable Estella quatercentenary number produced by these Madrid Franciscans some twelve years ago. The other is the *Estudis Franciscans*, published in Catalan by the Capuchin Fathers of Sarrià, near Barcelona, which has been in the forefront of Franciscan scholarship for over thirty years, and, one may hope, will prove to have been only temporarily suspended by the tragic happenings in Barcelona.

The Spanish Carmelites have perhaps done their country an even greater service through the truly monumental editions of Saint Teresa of Jesus, Saint John of the Cross and their contemporary Jerónimo Gracián given us by P. Silverio de Santa Teresa, O.C.D., to be followed, if circumstances permit, by editions of other Carmelite ascetics and mystics. Beside these should be placed the valuable critical studies of his younger fellow-Carmelite, P. Crisógono de Jesús Sacramentado, which hold out great promise for the future.

The Society of Jesus, of all the religious congregations, is "the most Spanish, by virtue of its foundation, of its history and of its eminent services both to culture in general and to the civilization of the Hispano-American nations."[1] Before its dissolution in Spain, in 1932, it maintained seventy houses and thirty colleges there, together with numerous social centres, working-men's clubs and benefit societies; and it has, of course, from almost the time of its foundation, been pre-eminent in missionary work abroad. Instead of trying in a page or two to compass all these activities I prefer to write of several of the better-known centres of Jesuit activity in Spain and show how much good work was done in each of them.

First, at Sarrià, that large suburb of Barcelona in which Capuchins and Salesians are also working, there was a group of Jesuit institutions well known in and beyond Spain. In the year in which it was closed the ecclesiastical college termed the Colegio Máximo had students of sixteen nationalities and the professors included many of world-wide fame in theological studies. In this College, which began in a small way at Tortosa in 1905 and was transferred to Sarrià ten years later, were incorporated three scientific foundations —an Institute of Chemistry, a School of Biology and a Laboratory of Experimental Psychology. P. Vitoria, founder of the first, and director of its seven laboratories, is the author of a large number of books and contributions to scientific reviews and for years he trained chemists and pharmacists and sent them to all parts of Spain. A similar success was attained by the Biological School under P. Pujiula, author of the first Spanish text-book on embryology, and by the Psychological Laboratory directed by P. Palmés. This, of course, was only one of the many activities of the Jesuits interrupted by the Republican Government in Barcelona, Spain's "second capital" and largest city. Attached to one of the Jesuit churches alone, the Sacred Heart, were five workmen's centres and schools in which rather more than

[1] *A.B.C.*, January 25, 1932. Cf. p. 145, below.

1,200 children, of both sexes, were being educated. Another parish had a school of 460 children, and several others, schools of between two and three hundred. The world-wide reputation of the Jesuits as educators makes it unnecessary to describe the curricula and methods of these schools in order to show that the teaching was of the first quality.

A second Jesuit Colegio Máximo is that of Oña—in the heart of the country, some thirty miles north-east of Burgos, which finds a place in guide-books chiefly on account of the remains of its Benedictine monastery, founded by Sancho the Great of Navarre. This was sacked in 1366 by the troops of the Black Prince who were fighting on behalf of Peter the Cruel and rebuilt soon afterwards with the addition of a wall and nine towers, which must have given it the appearance of a fortress. It is nearly sixty years since the Jesuits took over this building, restored the church and cloisters and built what rapidly became one of the most important colleges of its kind in Spain. Beginning with less than one hundred students, it had nearly three times that number in 1931. Oña specialized in philosophy and theology, though some of its professors were experts in other fields. There was the same broad curriculum as one finds in other Jesuit colleges; the new buildings, besides lecture-rooms and dormitories, included chemical and physical laboratories and a natural history museum, and the library contained some hundred thousand volumes. Two other Colegios Máximos demand mention—that of Comillas, a seaside resort near Santander, and that of Granada, the special study of which is astronomy.

Another aspect of the Jesuits' work in Spain was principally social. There was, for example, the Catholic Workers' Club, at Burgos, which, at the time of the dissolution of the Society, had 1,500 members, and was developing a housing estate on modern lines in the suburbs of the city. The same Club had a library, a savings bank, a benefit society, day and night classes for workers, and a school of arts and crafts.

At Valladolid, in the same part of Spain, there was a social centre, with a thousand members, many of them railwaymen, comprising recreation rooms, a cinema theatre, a co-operative society, a labour exchange, a printing press and a savings bank. This Centre was founded at the beginning of the twentieth century by P. Marcelino de Paz, who died in 1932, at the great age of ninety. P. Marcelino also founded a model reformatory, where boys with a bad record were trained for useful employments or skilled trades. At the time when the campaign against the religious Orders began, arrangements were being made for the enlargement of the reformatory and its transference to new buildings. This and similar plans were rudely interrupted; it is hard to estimate what Burgos and Valladolid, like other large cities, have suffered through the short-sighted policy of those who, in attacking religion, also attacked education, science, literature, art and social service.

Coming now to lesser Orders and Societies, some of them of comparatively recent foundation, we shall enquire what these are doing to promote elementary education, craftsmanship and culture among the middle and lower classes.

The Escuelas Pías, of which there are many in Italy, Germany, Hungary and other countries as well as in Spain, are a Spanish foundation dating from 1617. Their begetter, San José de Calasanz, was an Aragonese who found his vocation as an educationist and became (for his time) a very enlightened one. Adopting the principle that education should be universal, popular and free, he attempted to open schools under the auspices of existing Orders, but, finding this impracticable, he founded an Order of his own. In 1936, the *Escolapios*[1] had in Spain five of their fifteen

[1] This is the shortened form of their title ("Orden de los Clérigos regulares pobres de la Madre de Dios de las Escuelas Pías") by which they are always known.

provinces—Catalonia, Aragon, Castile, Valencia and Vas-
conia—60 houses, and 1,475 religious educating 29,900
children. Two of the schools—Moyà, in Catalonia, and
Peralta de la Sal, in Aragon—go back to the seventeenth
century and twenty to the eighteenth. All the education
which they give is free; the only fees paid are for board and
lodging, by about twenty per cent of the children. Besides
rendering this public service, the Escolapians supply many
of their poorer pupils with food and clothing; provide
savings banks for those with rather more means; and in the
summer organize *colonias escolares*, or holiday camps, in
the country.

Vocational education is not forgotten. At Sarrià the
Escolapians have a Commercial School, with a miniature
business office for instructional purposes, the first of its kind
in Spain. Other extensions of this type are the Escolapians'
Commercial Museum at Sarrià, their Botanical Gardens at
Getafe and their Madrid Observatory. They were largely
responsible, through P. Benito Feliú, for the restoration of
the University of Valencia, and played an important part,
through their school in that city, in the Valencian Renaissance of the nineteenth century. Among them are scholars
of repute—Hebraists, mathematicians, palaeographers—but
their central achievement is the contribution which they
make to elementary education, which, even at the low rate
of remuneration which education commands in Spain, saves
the State something like £100,000 per annum.

The Institute of the Brothers of the Christian Schools is
of French origin; it was founded at Rheims, by Saint Jean-
Baptiste de la Salle, in 1680. For a long time it remained
predominantly French; was suppressed during the Revolution and restored in 1802; and, at the beginning of the twentieth century, had 1,400 schools in France. Its extension
abroad began after the Law of 1904; and, as this was a period

in which Spain was feeling very keenly its backwardness in education, its growth there was rapid. By 1910 it had one hundred Spanish schools, and, twenty years later, the number had increased to 133, two-thirds of which were educating the children of the poor gratuitously. At the time when the Law of Religious Congregations was passed by the Republican Government, the total number of children receiving education from these Brothers was estimated at 40,000, over four-fifths of whom were holding free places. Twelve of the schools were situated in or very near Madrid, where elementary education, even under the Republic, was notoriously deficient: one of these was destroyed by fire in the riots of May 1931.

Both in Madrid and elsewhere, special attention has been paid by the Brothers to the education of the very poor, and, where one of their schools takes fee-paying pupils, it is a rule that such a school shall support another, in the same locality, at which no fees are taken. The Colegio de las Maravillas in Madrid, destroyed in 1931, united both types, approximately half its thousand pupils having been admitted gratuitously, most of them the children of working people in the populous suburb of Cuatro Caminos. It was the school itself which the incendiaries first attacked, before turning their attention to the laboratories, natural history museum and library—a strange way to make war on the Church, since it was the children of the working-classes who chiefly suffered!

The 133 Spanish schools of the Brothers included twelve secondary schools, four technical or vocational colleges, twenty-three commercial schools, three orphanages, twenty evening schools, eleven schools of the Salesian "festive oratory" type, and a number of institutions of the character of continuation schools, in which further instruction was given to past pupils. The Brothers are laymen and normally do no other work than teaching, apart from the production of text-books used in their classes. In the days before the persecution of the schools of the religious Orders began, the State used to employ these schools for practice work in the education course leading to the official Teachers' Diploma.

The majority of the Brothers' schools are situated in the poorer quarters of the great cities, in towns where little other elementary education is to be found, or in mining districts where there is a dense population over a comparatively small area. Many of the schools have been established by private benefaction—some by wealthy individuals who have chosen this method of helping the poor, knowing that their gifts will be well administered; others by industrial concerns which would hardly be accused of sentimentalism, and may, therefore, fairly be considered as witnesses to the efficiency of this kind of education.

A few examples will show how varied are the benefactors of the Christian Schools. At Santiago, in Galicia, the Brothers were entrusted with the organization and teaching in a school founded by the well-known business house of Simeón García. At Ujo, in Asturias, the school was originally founded for the children of workmen belonging to the Sociedad Hullera Española, and a number of similar schools in the mining districts of Asturias owe their origin to the same necessity and the lack of any other school to meet it. At Verín, in the north-western province of Orense, on the other hand, and at Llanes, on the Santander-Asturian boundary, the Brothers' schools were endowed by a type of millionaire very common in these northerly provinces—the man who in his youth has emigrated to Spanish America, and, having made his money, comes back to spend his last years at home. At Valladolid, the school was established by a local leather manufacturer; at Jerez, by Pedro Domecq, the famous wine merchant.

The largest of the schools is that of Nuestra Señora de la Bonanova, in one of the large suburbs of Barcelona, which

9

in 1931 had 1,100 pupils and for many years has drafted its best scholars into the secondary schools of Barcelona and the great industrial school at Tarrasa. But it is, perhaps, the smaller schools of the Brothers that are the most needed and have done the most valuable work, which, had they not been there, would not have been done at all.

Another group of lay brothers takes its title from a six-teenth-century Portuguese founder, Saint John of God. The hospitals of St. John of God in Spain date from shortly after their founder's death, when they were established in Castile and Andalusia under the patronage of the King who achieved the brief-lived union of Spain and Portugal, Philip II. Some twenty hospitals, asylums and sanatoria of this Order are now to be found in Madrid, Barcelona, Valencia, Granada and other large cities of Spain. Though I have never visited any of these, I have often heard, from those who know them well, of the devotion with which the Brothers nurse both children and adults afflicted with the most terrible physical and mental ailments. The best known of these institutions is probably the Asylum of San Baudilio de Llobregat, near Barcelona, which was taken over by the Brothers as long ago as 1895, and serves the most populous district in the whole country.

Brothers of the people, indeed, are these—brothers who educate, instruct, train, nurse, console and cheer the poor the infirm and all who need their care. Their work brings neither to themselves nor to their Orders any such great distinction as comes to the scholars of the religious Orders of which I first wrote. But it forms a firm foundation of charity and devotion without which Spain would be im-measurably poorer. Were these Orders driven from the country, were the endowments given specifically for their work diverted to other purposes, it may be doubted if the work itself would be performed by the State with the same efficiency, or even performed at all. It is certain that the spirit which animates it would have disappeared, and one must never forget that beneath the material prosperity of these institutions lies something far more important than up-to-date methods and effective results—a zeal derived from burning love.

The Society of Saint François de Sales was founded by St. John Bosco at Turin in 1859, and given its Rule and Constitutions by Pius XI fifteen years later. But the Saint's work among children began as early as 1844, so that the first of his "Oratories," as his special schools were termed, will soon reach its centenary. It should be noted that the great need for educational work in Spain, due to the neglect of it by the State, led to a more rapid development of the Salesian schools there than in most other countries. When their founder died, in 1888, there were fifty-seven in Europe and America combined, only two of which were in Spain. In 1910, on the death of the next Superior, the total number had been multiplied by six, but the number of Spanish houses had risen from two to twenty-nine. By 1921, Spain had thirty-eight houses; by 1931, fifty.

The spirit of the Society, expressed in its motto "Da mihi animas; caetera tolle," is nowhere better shown than in its "festive oratories," which are perhaps the best known of its institutions in Spain. The children who attend these on Sundays begin the day with the performance in common of their religious duties, and then play games (of which the favourite is usually that known as *fútbol*), practise in the gymnasium, sing or listen to vocal or instrumental music, attend illustrated talks in the theatre or see films in the cinema of the institution. As far as possible, the Fathers have aimed at working in places where they are most needed; these schools are attended by about twenty thousand children.

The "daily oratories"—free schools of the ordinary

primary type—have a total of about seventeen thousand scholars; in addition, some five thousand adolescents and adults attend the evening schools attached to them. Both by means of these latter, and by inviting parents and elder children to the Sunday theatres and cinemas, the Fathers keep in touch with the environments in which their children live. Of recent years past pupils have also formed their associations, and some six thousand adolescents remain under the direct influence of the Society through the body which federates these associations, publishing its own review and organizing a savings bank, a mutual assistance society and other beneficent activities. Some little while ago, the co-operative housing society formed by the association at Valencia, where the Salesians were particularly strong, had about one hundred houses in the "Bosco quarter" of the city. Quite a different type of activity, but one which derives directly from the sainted founder's habit of composing little plays for the children in his Oratories to act, is the publication of a large "Colección dramática" by the Salesians at Sarrià. Self-expression by means of drama was one of the most striking features in St. John Bosco's very progressive scheme of education, and this has always made a strong appeal to Spanish children, for Spaniards are particularly susceptible to impressions conveyed in dramatic form. The collection just referred to consists of over three hundred plays suitable for acting, some by adults and some by children; the same house has published several volumes of dialogues and poems for recitation, and an anthology of songs and short musical comedies, some thirty of which last were composed by one of the Fathers.

At Sarrià, too, the Salesians have their schools of arts and crafts: indeed, it is in their School of Typography that the books enumerated above are printed. Carpentry, drawing in all its branches, tailoring, bootmaking, carving, gilding, printing and binding are the principal subjects of instruction.

Some of these have been taught at Sarrià for over fifty years. The School of Typography is believed to be the oldest of its kind in Spain, and, since 1885, when it was established, the Salesians have founded seven more in the Peninsula and eighty in other countries of Europe or in America. They have also a number of schools of agriculture, a subject which is studied not only on its practical, but also on its theoretical side: the "Salesian Library of Agriculture," which they publish, consists of over forty volumes. How well their labours are spread over the country will be gathered from the fact that they have (or had) schools of arts and crafts at Madrid, Barcelona, Pamplona, Seville, Cádiz, Málaga and Valencia. A year or two ago, they were building what would have been the largest and most comprehensive of all at Bilbao: I have not heard if it ever began work in these recent years of turmoil or what has been its fate.

These details will be sufficient to show that, although the child leaves the Salesian oratory at fourteen, he is neither neglected nor forgotten after that age. His tastes and abilities are studied while he himself is studying and, once he has decided what trade or profession he wishes to follow, he is given all possible help, advice and training for it. This is an important point, because Spanish critics of the schools kept by the religious Orders sometimes talk as though boys and girls were unduly influenced and unconsciously trained for Church or cloister. Nothing could be farther from the truth. The Salesians, like the other religious who labour in Spain, aim at making their pupils, in whatever sphere they may work, good Christians and efficient Spaniards—that is to say, of the maximum benefit to their country.

Girls are not neglected by the Salesians, who have sixteen girls' schools of various types in Spain and train about two thousand working girls in trades such as those described above. In all types of school, the large majority of pupils and apprentices are admitted without fee. A few pay small sums—at Sarrià, for example, the maximum fee for board, lodging and tuition is sixty pesetas monthly. The Salesian schools suffered very greatly during the Second Republic, especially in the outbursts of May 1931, for it so happened that many of them were situated in the towns where most damage was done. Three—in Madrid, Valencia and Málaga —were burned down, and a second Madrid school, in the suburb of Tetuán, was assaulted, and would have suffered the same fate had not the men-folk of the three hundred girls who were being educated in it succeeded in dispersing the crowds. This was one of the brightest episodes of that tragic period and will be remembered as an example of the gratitude which the Spanish Salesians had earned in this country of their Order's adoption.

Finally, it must be remembered that for centuries the Orders have been giving of their best to missionary work, especially in Hispano-America. Here they follow the traditions of the Franciscans, the Dominicans and the Jesuits already referred to who were the first to evangelize the newly discovered continent and many of whom suffered martyrdom there. Of the 3,000 priests and their 1,300 helpers who were working in America when the latest statistics available were published ten years ago, a very large majority are members of religious congregations. The same may be said of the teachers in the 304 secondary schools and colleges supported by the Church, which between them have some 40,000 pupils. Statistics of the same date give the numbers of children in elementary schools supported by the Church in Spain as over 143,000, exclusive of orphanages whose inmates total 13,000. These figures, of course, have nothing to do with the religious activities in each of the countries concerned or of the religious Orders whose members are citizens of those countries. They refer solely to the missionary work of Spain, which, though having no longer any political connection with them, continues to lend its aid in the conversion and education of the people.

Nearly all the older Orders are represented in a long catalogue of these activities compiled some years ago to give a comprehensive idea of their wide diffusion. The Carmelites have missions in Colombia; the Augustinians, in Colombia and Peru; the Dominicans, in Peru and Ecuador; either the Franciscans or the Capuchins in Colombia, Venezuela, Ecuador, Chile, Argentina, Peru and Brazil. Brazil, though a Portuguese-speaking country, has also missions sent by the Benedictine, Dominican and Mercedarian Orders in Spain. The Society of Jesus has houses of residence or colleges in every one of the republics of Hispano-America: eleven houses, twelve colleges and two seminaries in Argentina, Chile and Colombia and eight houses and eight colleges in the other republics. The College of Belén, in Havana, built at a cost of ten million pesos, is the largest Jesuit College in the world. Nor do the Spanish religious Congregations in America confine themselves to evangelization, philanthropy and elementary education. Their observatories, laboratories, libraries and learned reviews are among the best in Hispano-America. Efficiency and scholarship characterize their activities abroad, as at home.

Still farther than to countries where their own language is spoken go the Spanish Orders. True to the earliest of the traditions of their Society, the Spanish Jesuits do a mighty work in China, where they are particularly successful in fostering vocations and training native Catholics for the priesthood. At Shanghai they have a Colegio Máximo and at Bombay a College affiliated to the University. They have also missions in outposts such as the Caroline, Marianne and Marshall Archipelagos, where not only have whole islands been christianized but native students are trained, before being sent to Manila to complete their education as missionaries to work among their brethren.

The Spanish Dominicans, too, are exceptionally active in Asia. In one entire Chinese province, in the Japanese island of Shikoku and in the island of Formosa, the Dominicans have entire spiritual jurisdiction and both here and elsewhere they have published native grammars, dictionaries and translations of the Bible and religious works, besides more ephemeral periodical publications of all kinds. Other centres of their work are Hong-Kong, where they alone keep the Spanish flag flying, and the Philippine Islands, where they have not only schools but a University of over three thousand students, all of which have to compete, and compete creditably, with American standards of efficiency.

Little has been said in these pages, for lack of space, of the religious Congregations more recently established in Spain. Let the Misioneros Hijos del Corazón de María serve as a single example. They are, as their title implies, a primarily missionary body. Some 700 of their 2,500 professed members work in America—chiefly in Argentina, Uruguay, Colombia and Brazil. They have houses in France, Germany, Italy and the United States. They maintain a seminary in China. But perhaps their greatest work is in Spanish Guinea. Here they have no less than 72 elementary and secondary schools, as well as a smaller but growing number of technical schools. The total number of schools built by the State is—eight! Since these religious went to Guinea in 1884 until the beginning of 1930 they received no grant from the State, which was just waking up to the importance of their work and beginning to subsidize it in return for the privilege of inspection, when the Law of Congregations put a stop, at least in theory, to its activities. I have no news of its history after 1932. No doubt the latest chapter will be not the least interesting when it comes to be written.

"How," asked a former pupil of an Augustinian college recently, "can we explain the apparently meaningless hatred of the religious Orders which seems to inspire some of our politicians? Have they not laboured, and do they not labour, ceaselessly and freely, in the interests of Spanish culture, both in Spain and abroad? Is the work of these scholars, critics, educators and missionaries nothing but a pious legend? Do not these literary and scientific works and institutions really exist—these books, in particular, of which the importance and value have been recognized again and again by men whose ideas are completely opposed to those of their authors? Are not these colleges, laboratories, libraries, reviews—above all, these thousands upon thousands of pupils and students who have benefited from them—palpable realities? And if we are told that no objection is taken to the religious as individuals, and that this eagerness to expel them from Spain comes only from the fact that they form parts of communities which are thought to be undesirable, is not the reply that as individuals they could never have done the great work which they have accomplished, for it is only when they are organized as a community that it becomes practically and economically possible?"

It is well said; and, to a reasonable and unprejudiced person, I think, it will seem unanswerable.

CHAPTER V

THE ORDERS AND THE SECOND REPUBLIC

WHEN, on April 14, 1931, King Alfonso XIII left his
country and the Provisional Government of the Second
Republic slipped quietly into the saddle, the hierarchy
of the Church in Spain must have realized that, without
the slightest doubt, the period of tranquillity which it
had enjoyed for some twenty years had come to an end.
Though Sr. Alcalá Zamora, the head of the new Government, was known to be a practising Catholic, several of his
colleagues were bitter enemies of the Church, and there
was every reason to fear, not merely a change in ecclesiastical policy that would wreck the 1851 Concordat, but,
following the traditions of Spanish politics, an emotional as
well as a political reaction of the most violent type, com-
parable perhaps to that of 1833 or 1868. Indeed, even
worse might have been feared, since Anarchism, with its
anti-God principles, was stronger now in Spain than ever
before, and Communism, the attitude of which to religion
is sufficiently notorious, was making steady progress. Both
Anarchism and Communism had been proscribed during
the seven-years' Dictatorship which had just ended; and
Spain, according to the Dictator's ideas, had been thoroughly swept and garnished. But many of those affected
by the proscription had spent the period of the Dictatorship
in Russia; and, on their return, had brought with them
seven other spirits worse than themselves, so that the last
state of the country was likely to be worse than the first. If
political attacks were made on the Church by the new
Government, the exaltation of the mobs, now inspired, not
merely by dislike of the clergy but by hatred of, or at least

126

disbelief in, God, might be expected to reach heights previously unknown. The perspective was a tragic one to contemplate and it would not have been surprising if the hierarchy had exhorted Catholics to oppose the new *régime* from the beginning—a step which could only have had the result of precipitating the civil war that King Alfonso had left Spain to avoid.

For, of course, the Second Republic had not the slightest claim to be regarded as anything but a *coup d'état* which had the one virtue essential to all *coups d'état*—that of having been successful. It came in under the disguise of legitimacy; but, once the emotions aroused by its advent had subsided, the thinness of the disguise became obvious. The elections which brought it in were not parliamentary but municipal; and the only results of these elections to be published showed a majority for the Monarchists of 22,150 seats over 5,875.[1]

The Republic came, not by the will of the entire people but by the will of three or four large cities where it had majorities and by the act of the King and his advisers who allowed it a trial in order to save the nation from war. All these facts, and others, the hierarchy might have adduced had it desired to lead a crusade against a *régime* which, humanly speaking, could not fail to be prejudicial to the Church. Viewed in the cold light of a later day the facts are undeniable, and many who look back dispassionately on the situation may be forgiven for wondering if the Church's leaders would not have done better to take a different line from the first.

But, for good or for evil, they judged it best to adopt a more generous view and to give the Republic, whether or no they approved of it as individuals, their unequivocal and official support. There were good reasons for their doing so. First, the *ancien régime* had refused battle when the *coup d'état* was struck, and a crusading rally is robbed of

[1] *The Spanish Tragedy*, p. 26.

much of its fervour when its champion has left the country without waiting for it to begin. Next, and as a consequence of this, the *nouveau régime* had come in peaceably, without violence or bloodshed, and was in undisputed possession. Then, even within the ranks of the clergy, opinions were divided on the question of republicanism *versus* monarchism: many of the inferior clergy believed that the Republic would raise the miserable stipends of parish priests as well as the miserable wages of peasants; it was even rumoured that there were dignitaries of the Church who believed that the economic salvation of Spain could never come under the Monarchy.

There was, of course, nothing whatever about a republican form of government to which a Catholic need, or even could, take exception. Catholicism is a form of religion; republicanism a form of government; and in the course of history the two have frequently got on perfectly well together. Therefore "we shall respect the Republican Government," ran the leading article in the principal Catholic organ of Spain, *El Debate*, on April 15, 1931, "not passively . . . but loyally and actively, doing all we can to help it in its mission." "The Church as such," wrote Cardinal Gomá, a month later, foreshadowing the language of an Encyclical of 1933, *Dilectissima Nobis*, "has no preference for one form of government above another. . . . The Church is neither monarchical nor republican; it is either, according to place and time, since it collaborates with both. . . . The Spanish Republic has done anything but help the Church . . . but, even if in any point its political doctrine is unacceptable, there is no question about its authority when legitimately exercised. . . . Therefore . . . it can demand both our respect and our collaboration."[1]

---

[1] Gomá, *op. cit.*, II, 106, 113, 115, 116. By an ironical chance these words were written on May 10, 1931, the day of the first church-burnings which took place under the Second Republic. There is a great deal more in this volume of the same tenor. Mendizábal (pp. 116–17) quotes from pastorals of the Archbishop of Valencia and the Bishop of Barcelona recommending "respect," "honour," and "loyal co-operation."

These quotations, which might be many times multiplied, are typical of the attitude of exemplary correctness taken up by the hierarchy and the Catholic Press during the five years of the Second Republic. At the outset, their position was that, since the Republican Government had, without opposition or violence, assumed power, it was the duty of Catholics to render obedience to it as to the lawfully constituted authority. If any Republican government should make war upon Christian principles or upon the Catholic Church it would become the duty of Catholics to work and vote against it; but that situation could be dealt with if and when it arose.

It was not long in arising. Less than a month after the coming of the Republic, the Church found itself in the grip of a persecution which continued at intervals until the fall of the left-wing Government in the autumn of 1933 and began again immediately upon the victory of the Popular Front in the elections of February 1936. On some of the phases of this persecution, such as the expulsion from Spain of Cardinal Segura,[1] I do not propose to dwell: they are narrated with sufficient fullness in *The Spanish Tragedy*. I would rather concentrate upon the persecution of the religious Orders; for it is they, representing the quintessence of Catholic devotion, both to God and to their fellow-men, that have been singled out to bear the brunt of their enemies' attack.

It was understood from the first that the Republic would disestablish the Church—and there were many Catholics, with a wide knowledge of Church life in other countries, who thought that the advantages of this outweighed its inconveniences. It seemed likely, too, that the equivalent of disendowment (already, as we have seen, pretty thoroughly carried out) would be voted—*i.e.*, that the clergy would lose the stipends guaranteed to them under Article 42 of the 1851

---

[1] *The Spanish Tragedy*, pp. 52–3, 58–9.

Concordat as compensation for past expropriations of Church property. This was a more questionable proceeding —a unilateral repudiation of the Concordat, without previous notice—which, as it chanced, was proposed to the Cortes, with ironic inappropriateness, by the Minister of Justice. The step was defended by its advocates on the ground that the State had already paid far more in stipends than the total value of the stolen property. A good deal might be said on this,[1] and on the unilateral repudiation of treaties in general, especially as Article 45 of the Concordat stipulates that it shall "hold good henceforth for ever in (Spanish) dominions, each of the contracting parties here promising, for itself and its successors, faithfully to observe each and every one of the articles which it contains," and the 1860 Convenio had provided that "at no time and in no eventuality" should the ecclesiastical stipends voted as compensation for the State's depredations be "reduced or diminished." But even as to this some held that, though the measure might be unjust, and, if not carefully graduated over a long period, inhuman, the moral and spiritual gain to the Church would in the long run be considerable.[2]

Both these measures were passed six months after the coming of the Republic, and, long before this, the Provisional Government had decreed the secularization of cemeteries, the immunity of individuals from penalties on account of their religious beliefs, complete freedom for non-Catholic worship and various other measures which not only eased life for the few Protestants and the larger number of free-thinkers and agnostics to be found in Spain, but encouraged those who were in a position to do so to excite prejudice against Catholicism.[3] So, from April 1931 onwards, one

---

[1] See, for example, Gomá, *op. cit.*, I, 216–17.
[2] Cf. p. 40, above.
[3] On the other hand, the Government prohibited foreigners from becoming ministers of churches or superiors of congregations, and this (cf. p. 5, above) hit the Spanish Protestants very hard. Cf. Araujo and Grubb, p. 51: "As regards evangelicals the actual position will probably only be resolved in

began to hear of practising Catholics, who took no part in political activities and were indeed quite uninterested in them, losing their employment for no other reason than the vaguely comprehensive one of "incompatibility with the *régime*."

At the beginning of May came the persecution and expulsion from Spain of Cardinal Segura, and, a few days afterwards, the first explosion of violence against the Church and particularly against the religious Orders, the nature and extent of which might alone have led observers to suspect that something more than anti-clericalism had inspired it, even if they had known nothing of Anarchism and Communism. As in 1834, so in 1931, the riots began in Madrid; and as then, so now, the Society of Jesus was the first to suffer. The Jesuit church and *residencia* in the Calle de la Flor, with the latter's magnificent library, were burned to the ground, and onlookers in sympathy with the incendiaries prevented the firemen from intervening. The great new church and monastery built by the Discalced Carmelites in the Plaza de España was next set alight. Then came the turn of the Jesuit *residencia* and Institute of Arts and Industries in Alberto Aguilera and the Mercedarian monastery in Bravo Murillo. Next, detachments of incendiaries went out to the suburbs and set fire to the College of Maravillas in Cuatro Caminos and that of the Sacred Heart in Chamartín. On the same morning several other buildings were fired but only partially destroyed. It will be noticed that religious houses rather than parish churches were the first objects of attack. Monks, friars and nuns were turned upon the streets and some of them would have remained out all night but for the charity of passers-by.

On the same day similar riots began in the south. Málaga suffered most: twenty-two churches and religious houses

practice. Foreign missionaries can no longer be ministers of churches, though it seems probable that they will be able to continue to work as evangelists. But warning may well be taken from the situation in Mexico where similar legislation has seriously hampered the work of the missionary."

were burned and twenty-six pillaged: priceless paintings by
Alonso Cano and sculptured groups by Pedro de Mena and
Francisco Zarcillo were among the treasures that vanished.
At Alicante, five religious houses were sacked and seven
destroyed by fire. At Orihuela and Albacete, monks and
nuns were evicted from their houses by the municipalities
and driven from the province. At Alicante, according to
an eye-witness of the devastation, "the Jesuit residence
. . . was the first attacked, but, owing to its central position
in a narrow street, it could not be burned without grave
danger to the whole town. The incendiaries, however, were
not to be robbed of their prey; by means of the pickaxe and
sledge-hammer the house was left a complete ruin. When
they had finished their work, nothing remained but a roofless
shell."[1] At Alicante railway-station, whence this writer
travelled to Barcelona, he met a nun, "a member of a small
community, Sisters of Charity, who directed a hospice for
the dying, a hospital for the poor and a leper colony in a
village outside Alicante. According to her story the incendiaries rushed into the hospital, threw the nuns on the floor
and brutally kicked them down the stairs."[2] This would
seem to be a somewhat extreme form of anti-clericalism.

Seville, Cádiz, Valencia, Granada, Murcia, Córdoba—
all the large cities of the south—suffered in these riots.
They were soon over. Within a week all was quiet again—
save men's minds. For the incendiaries had shown of what
horrors they were capable and the Government had tacitly
indicated that they might be committed with impunity.
For no account ever appeared of the punishment of anyone
in connection with them; indeed, the official statements
which appeared in the Press must rather have encouraged
them than not, for the Government declared that at bottom
it was all the fault of the Monarchists![3]

[1] T. J. O'Donnell in *Studies* (Dublin), September 1931.   [2] *Ibid.*
[3] *The Spanish Tragedy*, p. 57.

Many of the accounts of these deplorable events stress the smallness of the attacking forces: sometimes, it is true, they were numerous, and a larger mob, which accompanied them, prevented the police from interfering; but often no more than a score of men would set fire to a church while hundreds of bystanders would watch the proceedings with an air of complete indifference. The inference wrongly drawn by some critics from such a scene is that the people were, in fact, indifferent to the fate of their churches. The correct inference is that the Government was indifferent, for in these large cities there was no lack of civil guards and armed police and the malefactors could perfectly well have been arrested and given exemplary punishment had not the Government feared that such a proceeding would arouse extremists all over the country and provoke that proletarian revolution which it was the avowed aim of all the extremist parties of the Left, profoundly as they differed one from another, to set in motion. What could a couple of hundred onlookers do, one may well ask, largely women and children as they were, against a score of armed and organized incendiaries? But what, it is even more relevant to enquire, could they be expected to do, when the guardians of law and order themselves stood by, unable or unwilling to intervene? The truth is, as anyone who talked freely with Spaniards about this time will remember, that the people were completely stupefied by the suddenness and the savagery of this initial outburst. When they became used to the idea that in future they would have to be prepared for attacks on churches, the parishes lost no time in arranging for armed guards to be on duty at times of unrest, and some of the most valuable possessions of the churches were removed to places of greater safety. But in May 1931 no one had suspected that such things were likely to happen. Only the ancient inhabitant could remember the church-burnings of the First Republic, and, except during the

Tragic Week in Barcelona,[1] which was twenty-two years old, there had been no large-scale incendiarism since. If they had been to school they had read of such things; or possibly they had heard their fathers or grandfathers talk about them. But that was history: so remote that it was never thought of in connection with the present day. And further, the tranquillity which had attended the advent of the Republic had put people completely off their guard. To the ordinary citizen the events of May 1931 came with the force of some terrible catastrophe: men talked of them as if they heralded some unheard-of series of disasters.

And so they did.

But much was to happen before the worst disaster came. There were, for example, the June elections, the first to be held under the Republic. Though these have no direct bearing on our main subject, it may be worth while, as an illustration of the correctness of the attitude taken up by the Spanish hierarchy, to quote a few passages *verbatim* from the episcopal declaration issued some days before the elections and exactly one month after the disgraceful events just recorded. It will be observed how fearlessly, yet how temperately, they speak of these, and also how strictly they limit the advice they give to what concerns their office.

> The Spanish Metropolitans have met in order to study calmly the situation created for the Church by the new order of things and to dictate. . . . the present collective pastoral declaration, which may serve Spanish Catholics as a common basis for judgment and action.
>
> The Bishops have absolutely nothing to do with the conflicts of political parties, and, as is laid down by ecclesiastical discipline, they have only to attend to the spiritual welfare of the faithful who are committed to their charge and to defend the sacrosanct and inalienable

---

[1] Where, as it happened, no riots took place in 1931. Cf. *Catalonia Infelix*, p. 205.

rights of the Church which, on the day of their consecration, they solemnly swore to maintain inviolate.

Each and every one of the Spanish prelates have already reminded the faithful of the duties which bind them to the constituted authorities and the obligation which is incumbent upon them to co-operate for the common good and for the maintenance of social order. The Spanish Metropolitans, at this their new meeting, fully ratify these statements, having confidence that the authorities will respect the rights of the Church, and of Catholics, in a nation in which the Catholic religion is professed by practically the entire population.

At the present time, when the nation is about to declare its will through the Constituent Cortes shortly to be elected, the prelates would not be fulfilling the gravest of obligations imposed upon them by their office if they did not recall to Spanish Catholics, together with the duty . . . of respecting and obeying the constituted authorities, other most urgent duties . . . which at this period of such great importance for our country and Church are incumbent upon them. . . .

It is the strictest duty of Spanish Catholics to take such active part in the approaching elections as the laws permit. . . . Further, it is of pressing moment that they should for the time lay aside their political preferences, which they are quite free to retain, and should effectively and seriously unite so that those candidates may be elected to the Constituent Cortes who give a clear pledge to defend the rights of the Church and of the social order.

In their sincere desire not to create difficulties for the Provisional Government, the Spanish prelates have until now kept silence, in the hope that it would respect all the rights which on so many grounds are enjoyed by the Church in Spain. But their silence might easily be interpreted as acquiescence in certain measures taken by the authorities and in events of the gravest character which have produced the most painful impression upon Catholics. . . . In emphatically denouncing these measures and these events, on which the Metropolitans will submit a memorandum to the President of the Provisional Government, they still cherish the hope that the Government, in accordance with the desires which it has so often expressed for peace and concord, will neither attempt nor allow any attack on the Church and its rights without first coming to an agreement with the Holy See.[1]

The Church, claimed the Spanish Bishops in 1937, "ranged itself resolutely on the side of the constituted authorities and endeavoured to collaborate with them for the common good. And despite the repeated commission of offences against persons, property and rights of the Church, it never swerved from its purpose of non-interference with the long-established *régime* of harmony with the State."[2] That is an absolutely correct and fair statement of a fact which it is right should be recognized from this point onward in our survey.

The elections over, the Cortes assembled to fashion the new Republican Constitution. The first draft of this was published at midsummer; the final draft was approved and promulgated in December. Between those two dates the Republican Government—that pathetic Government of good intentions and lost opportunities—flung aside conciliatory and generous action and committed itself irrevocably to a programme of persecution, described by the Spanish Bishops without the slightest exaggeration as "one continuous and violent attack upon the national conscience."[3]

To those familiar with their history it came as no great surprise to find in the draft Constitution a provision that "the State shall dissolve all the religious Orders and shall nationalize their property." But it was a terrible shock to the ordinary Spaniard, who knew little or nothing of the

---

[1] *El Sol*, June 12, 1931. Cf. a similar passage in Gomá (Pastoral: "Sobre los deberes de la hora presente"), III, 31–2.
[2] *Joint Letter*, p. 4.   [3] *Joint Letter*, p. 8.

attacks made on the Church throughout the nineteenth century but realized the untold benefits which the Orders had brought to Spain. Whether he was a devout and instructed man who could understand what was meant by the contemplative life; or a learned man, who recognized and had profited by the services of the Orders to learning; or a family man, who was depending upon them to educate his children; or a poor man, whom they had clothed and saved from hunger; or merely a fair-minded man, who saw no reason why a Government professing Liberal principles should treat a body of harmless people so illiberally—in any of these cases, he was appalled at the light-heartedness with which this new Republic proposed to expel some of its worthiest citizens. But it is probably inexact to say that, on mature reflection, he was gravely perturbed about this article. If he knew anything about politics, he knew that the Prime Minister, Sr. Alcalá Zamora, and the Home Secretary, Don Miguel Maura, were good Catholics, and he trusted to their influence to prevent such a disaster. If he were ignorant of politics—as many Spaniards are—he trusted—as all Spaniards do—to luck. And to some extent his confidence was justified.

Many members of the Cortes were determined that the Orders should go. Many others were determined that they should not. And among the latter were ministers, or members whose opinion carried great weight, who, though not themselves practising Catholics, were fully conscious of the usefulness and worth of the Orders and fully sensible of the importance of not alienating the large body of conservative opinion in the country to a greater extent than was unavoidable. Many conversations were held between representatives of groups and parties long before the question was debated on the floor of the House. And in the end it was decided that history should yet again repeat itself and that the Jesuits should be sacrificed.

It may perhaps be worth while to transcribe those parts of the article of the Constitution as finally passed (Article 26) which relate to the religious Orders:

All religious confessions shall be considered as Associations subject to a special law.

The State, regions, provinces and municipalities shall neither maintain nor favour nor grant financial aid to religious institutions, associations and churches. . . .

Those religious Orders are dissolved which besides the three canonical vows statutorily impose a further special vow of obedience to an authority other than the legitimate authority of the State. Their property shall be nationalized and devoted to educational and beneficent purposes.

The remaining religious Orders shall become subject to a special law voted by these Constituent Cortes and laid down on the following bases:

1. Dissolution of those whose activities make them a danger to the safety of the State;[1]

2. Registration of those which are to remain, a special register being kept for this purpose by the Ministry of Justice;

3. Incapacity to acquire and hold, either directly or through any intermediary, property other than that which they have previously proved to be necessary for their own subsistence or for the direct fulfilment of their particular ends.

4. Prohibition to practise industry, commerce or teaching.

5. Submission to all the tributary laws of the country.

6. Obligation to render annual accounts to the State of the investment of their wealth in relation with the aims of their Association.

---

[1] The opportunity for persecution which this clause gave any Government that might wish for it need not be emphasized. "The freedom which it allows the Cortes," remarked Sr. Azaña during the debate on the article (October 8, 1931), "could not be greater. . . . All the Orders, or none of them, will now be dissoluble, exactly as the Cortes may desire."

It shall be permissible for the property of the religious Orders to be nationalized.

One had the feeling, after studying this article, that the fable of the wolf and the lamb was likely to be re-enacted before Spain was much older. First, if a suitable accusation could be found, the Orders might be faced with the necessity for justifying their allegiance to Rome. If this were satisfactorily done, they might then be called upon to prove that their activities did not endanger the safety of the State. Then a charge might be brought against them of holding property not essential to their subsistence. Or some of their charitable or educational activities might be interpreted as being industrial or commercial. Or a clever lawyer (and there are so many lawyers in Spain!) might pick holes in their accounts. Or at the very worst, charges against them might be based on the terms of the 1851 Concordat ("If it wasn't you," said the wolf, "it was your father, and it's all the same thing!"), in which case that convenient final sentence in the Article was standing ready to legitimize confiscation of their property without further formality. . . .

It was, in fact, a famous victory. If the Church's most determined enemies failed to get the whole of their desires, they certainly got as near to them as made little matter.

The debate on Article 26, however, did provoke a crisis, and a serious one. I have already summarized the main arguments employed in defence of the Article:[1] the amazing contention of Sr. Azaña, then War Minister, that "Spain has ceased to be Catholic"; his frank admission of the illiberality of the proposals and his subordination of liberal principle to expediency; the expressions of admiration which the work of the Orders wrung from the very Minister who led the campaign against them; the singling out of the Society of Jesus as the Republican scapegoat; and the

---

[1] *The Spanish Tragedy*, pp. 70–73.

139

attempt made to defend the prohibition of teaching by the
Orders with the argument that their teaching is "contrary
to the principles which are the foundation of the modern
State." In a book on this subject, it may perhaps be permissible to quote from the verbatim report of the paragraph
in which Sr. de los Ríos paid a spontaneous tribute to the
work of two of them:

> The religious problem . . . is the deepest and most
> intimate problem that exists in Spanish life. The House
> must make a distinction within this apparent unity of
> the religious Congregations and Orders. Do not forget—
> and I take this merely as an example—that among them
> are the Sisters of Charity and the Brethren of St. John of
> God. In the presence of these communities one forgets
> all discrepancies of dogma; one can see nothing but a
> witness of the abnegation of which souls fired with love
> are capable. I say, gentlemen, that it is essential for us to
> make a distinction, for when we are faced with instances
> of that kind the dogmatic problem disappears and there
> remains only the common denominator of humanity and
> the recognition of what a fervent soul is capable of in the
> sphere of sacrifice. . . .[1]

This tribute, we learn from the report in *El Sol*, called forth
"great applause and acclamation from almost all parts of
the House," two deputies who attempted to interrupt the
speaker being silenced by "protests from a great many
members."

The Article was passed, as it could hardly fail to be, since
enthusiasm for the newly born Republic had sent to the
Cortes an enormous left-wing majority. But, remarkable to
say, hardly more than half the left-wing members were
present for the division, and the figures showed no more
than 178 supporters and 59 dissentients in a House whose

---

[1] *El Sol*, October 9, 1931.

full effective strength at that time was over 460. Even the Government treated its own proposals with some indifference. One of the Ministers who voted for it declared that he did so only because the alternative was the dissolution of all the Orders.[1] Three more who might have been expected to vote for it were absent; and two—the Prime Minister and the Home Secretary—voted against it and immediately afterwards resigned their offices. This last event gave the presidency of the Government to Sr. Azaña, who thus gained the distinction of being the protagonist in the campaign against the Church during the Republic's first biennium.

The most contentious of its articles safely passed, the rest of the Constitution was slowly disposed of, the handful of right-wing deputies who were true to Catholic principles challenging valiantly and vainly articles as repugnant to Catholics as those on marriage and divorce. Talk of a revisionist campaign headed by the late Prime Minister was rife during November, but it came suddenly to an end with the announcement that the late Prime Minister had not thought it inconsistent with his resignation to accept the Presidency of the Republic, with a salary of one million pesetas per annum and another million and a quarter for expenses. In December he was elected, and immediately afterwards the Radicals left the Government, which now became predominantly Socialist, and inaugurated what was popularly known as the "red biennium."

Yet even with this Government in power, and with a Constitution containing so much that was offensive to Catholics, the hierarchy maintained the same loyalty to the Republic as it had shown before the June elections. In a pastoral written on August 29, 1931, when the publication of the draft Constitution had revealed the spoliatory designs of the Constituent Cortes, Cardinal Gomá contrasted the

---

[1] *The Spanish Tragedy*, pp. 93–4.

Church's "frank and noble attitude of deference to the present *régime* with the inconsiderate disdain and legal persecution" to which the Republic had subjected it. He then continued in these striking words:

> You will remember that, at the time of the change of *régime* . . . we exhorted you, in the interests of the common weal, to pay all respect to the constituted authority. Our duty fulfilled, we need have done no more. But a few days later we addressed you a Pastoral Letter entitled "The duties of the present time" . . . telling you that your obligation, and the obligation of all, was, without renouncing your private opinion on forms of government, to collaborate with the men of the new *régime*.
>
> And we still say the same, and for so long as there is breath in our body we shall continue to do so. The authority set over us comes from God, even though the men in whom it is incarnated should profess to dispense with God; and we must submit to it in reason and in will for so long as its bearings (*orientaciones*) and its commands do not run counter, in our consciences, to the authority and the commands of God.[1]

Nor did the loyalty of the hierarchy waver when its all but worst fears were fulfilled and its patience was tried to the utmost. A collective statement issued on December 20, 1931, after condemning the legislation already referred to, recalls the "respect and obedience" which Christians owe to constituted authority even when that authority is abused by those who wield it. Spanish Catholics must therefore continue to respect the civil powers. The Church must not be identified with any one party nor must Catholic interests be subordinated to the victory of such a party even if it would be likely to work for the defence of religion. Above all, into whatever troubles the Church may be plunged,

[1] Gomá, II, 177.

Catholics must not think of taking vengeance. The Church must answer iniquity with justice and overcome evil with good.

"These directions," remarks an impartial commentator, "were clear enough . . . and given in eminently Christian language. Would they assuage party resentment, hate and rancour?"[1] That was what remained to be seen.

At the beginning of 1932 came the next attack of the Government on the religious Orders. This consisted in the application of the third of the above-quoted clauses of Article 26 to the Society of Jesus and the dissolution of the Society on Spanish territory. A decree dated January 23, 1932, appointed the dissolution to take place on February 3. The President of the Republic had apparently no scruples in signing the decree without comment and within a fortnight of its promulgation the Jesuits were leaving the country.[2]

In the heat of the Cortes debate, some of those who voted for the short-sighted and illiberal Article may honestly have believed that the Society of Jesus came under the heading of "Orders which, besides the three canonical vows, statutorily impose a further special vow of obedience to an authority other than the legitimate authority of the State." But they could certainly not plead ignorance when the Article in question was officially applied to the Jesuits. On January 15, the Spanish Press published a long and closely reasoned letter from the Provincials of the Society to the Prime Minister, enclosing a juridical declaration drawn up by five leading lawyers and endorsed by a large number of others, which clearly shows that, whatever the intentions of those who promoted it may have been, the Article, as passed by the Cortes, did not properly characterize the obligations which the Society imposes.

[1] Mendizábal, p. 174, who reproduces in a French translation (pp. 172–4) the main points of this document.
[2] *The Spanish Tragedy*, p. 95.

The Jesuits, declared the document, all take "the three vows of poverty, chastity and obedience to their superiors," and, in addition, "the professed, who, according to the data furnished, number less than ten per cent of the total membership" of the Society, take an additional vow according to the formula presented by St. Ignatius and approved by Paul III (1540) and by Julius III (1550). This says that, "for the greater humiliation of our Society and the perfect mortification of each one of us and the abnegation of our wills," we bind ourselves "to accomplish that which the Pontiff of to-day or his successors may command, in whatsoever concerns the welfare of souls, and the propagation of the faith, and any missions to which they may be pleased to send us."

This undertaking, the document proceeds, is a ratification—an "underlining," as it were—of the vow of obedience taken by all the Orders, in no sense envisaging any submission to an authority which may prevent lawful obedience being paid to the State. The very Article tacitly recognizes the permissibleness of the vow of obedience "to the spiritual power of the Roman Pontiff, whom all Catholics must obey," and only when it is explicitly referred, by those who take it, to the welfare of souls or the propagation of the faith, does the new Constitution consider it illegal.

After quoting a recent letter from Cardinal Pacelli to the General of the Jesuits (*Acta Apostolicae Sedis*, November 9), which expressly defines the obedience promised by this vow as "that which all Catholics, and, more particularly, all religious, owe to the Holy See," the signatories to this document proceed to show from the Canons that all religious, and all priests, of the Catholic Church are bound to the Holy Father in exactly the same way as that in which the Jesuits, as an act of humiliation, bind themselves, and that therefore the vow is properly an act of humiliation only. Concluding with a plea for religious liberty, addressed to the head of a

Government which has professed to stand for religious liberty, the declaration asserts that to dissolve the Society of Jesus in Spain will be a measure of pure injustice, since under the new Constitution the Society has as much right to exist in the country as has any other religious Order.

It was noteworthy that the Press received the dissolution decree with marked coldness. The right-wing Press, as it happened, had been muzzled by the recent suspension of the Catholic newspaper *El Debate*—this under a Government which stood for the freedom of the Press—and that sturdy defender of the Church, *A.B.C.*, could only "content itself with placing its protest on record in a sober fashion."[1]

> The decree contravenes the principles of freedom of worship and freedom of conscience. It contravenes the rights connected with property established by the Constitution and sets up confiscatory proceedings which the Constitution itself condemns. And by its application of an absolutely erroneous hypothesis concerning the extra-national vow, it forbids the right of association to a genuinely Spanish community—the most Spanish of all the Congregations, by virtue of its foundation, of its history and of its eminent services to culture in general and to the civilization of the Hispano-American nations.

As an example of the unpopularity of the decree with those who supported the party responsible for it, we may take the Catalan left-wing newspaper *La Publicitat*, at that time the staunchest friend of Sr. Azaña's Government. Its leading article, on January 26, ran thus:

> The decree now published can surprise no one, though it is arousing protests which we ourselves recognize as logical. . . . As Liberals, we are opposed to all that impedes the exercise of individual rights, and for that

[1] January 25, 1932.

145

reason we entirely deprecate the illiberal nature of Article 26 and the decree which is the result of it.[1]

But perhaps the most telling of all the purely political protests against the decree came from the Barcelona organ of the right-wing autonomist party (Lliga Catalana), *La Veu de Catalunya*.[2] It began with a recall to realism. "Everywhere there are strikes, conflicts and rehearsals for a social revolution and for the overthrow of the constituted order. The Government announces that these Anarchist or Communist movements are revolutionary in character and even . . . that they are a prelude to this attack which is being planned and prepared." One would have thought, continued the writer, that in these circumstances the Government would have done all in its power to unite the various forces which are opposed to such a revolution. But it was doing just the contrary. "At the very moment of a revolutionary strike it issues a decree dissolving the Society of Jesus and confiscating its property, on the grounds that its members take a fourth vow of obedience to an authority other than the legitimate authority of the State. The pretext could not be more puerile. Associations are allowed to exist and function which are affiliated to the Socialist International, the Communist International and the Anarchist International, associations whose aim is the destruction of the State, the country and the family. . . . Does the Government wish to break all the bonds which keep our society together?"

It was an apt question. Day after day, in every town in Spain, these revolutionary organizations were being allowed to hold up public business and to boast openly that their strikes were rehearsals for the proletarian revolution. And instead of directing its energies against these would-be disruptors of society the Government of Sr. Azaña occupied

[1] January 26, 1932.   [2] January 27, 1932.

itself in disbanding an organization which not only had never encouraged or supported revolution of any kind but stood and worked actively for the maintenance of those social institutions on which the life of the country was founded.

Had it not been so tragic, it would have been ridiculous.

The Society was duly dissolved. Most of the Fathers left the country, to take up their work elsewhere, though a few remained, as they had of course every right to do, in their private capacity. None doubted that they would be re-instated, as they had been in the past, so soon as this particular attack upon the Church had spent itself.[1] But meanwhile their churches, residences, schools and colleges were confiscated and turned to secular uses.

During the spring and summer of 1932, the Government was occupied with the Agrarian Law and the Catalan Autonomy Statute and with the suppression not only of Anarchist and Communist exuberance but of the only revolt which came from the right wing during the Republican quinquennium.[2] In October it prepared for a new attack on the religious Orders which was embodied in the notorious "Law of Religious Congregations and Confessions."

This was the "special law" referred to in the 1931 Constitution to which all religious communities remaining in Spain were to be required to submit. Much of it merely confirmed or amplified Articles 26 and 27 of the Constitution. The first section guaranteed "freedom of conscience and worship," declared that the State had no "official religion" and forbade confessions to worship outside their own buildings, save with Governmental sanction. The second section allowed all confessions to appoint their own officers

---

[1] A Protestant view may be worth quoting. "The Jesuit contribution to higher education was a very notable one in Spain. . . . The wisdom of such a dissolution may . . . be questioned on many grounds." (Araujo and Grubb, p. 48).

[2] *The Spanish Tragedy*, pp. 117–19.

and ministers, provided these were Spaniards, though, "should a person be elected who might be a danger to the order or safety of the State," he would not be recognized by it. The third section declared that the property of religious bodies belongs to the State, "under whose safeguard" (ironic words, as events proved!) they are held. Much follows about inventories, taxation and the right of the State to dispose of such property. "The State will encourage the creation of museums for ecclesiastical bodies" (this sounds sepulchral, but so the phrase runs). Any property acquired by religious corporations after the promulgation of the law may be held by them as private property but only so far as is necessary for religious ends. They may "found and direct establishments for the giving of instruction in their respective doctrines and for the training of their ministers," but the State, by means of inspection, will see that none of these "teach doctrines which threaten the safety of the Republic."

The most contentious section of the Law was the final one, which dealt with the religious Orders. These, under pain of dissolution at the will of the Cortes, must exercise "no kind of political activity." All Orders—now technically "Associations"—must submit copies of their statutes, a statement of the "aims" of each of their "houses or residences," an inventory of their possessions, the names of their superiors (who must be Spanish), the names of their members (at least two-thirds of whom must be Spanish) and a list of the possessions which each member has brought to the Order. These details must be kept up to date, and each "house or residence" must submit its books and annual balance sheet for inspection. A member of an Order may at any time abandon it, "notwithstanding any vow or promise to the contrary," under State protection. In such an eventuality, the Order "shall be obliged to return to him all that he has brought or ceded to it," with a reasonable deduction corresponding to the time he has spent in the Order.

Finally, no Order may engage, either directly or through an intermediate party, in "commerce, industry or agricultural exploitation," though it may grow food for its own consumption. No Order, apart from training its own members, may engage in teaching, and State inspection of schools will prevent the formation of secondary schools by the Orders through the intermediacy of lay folk. All teaching by members of religious Orders must come to an end by October 1, 1933, except in elementary schools, for which the period is extended until December 31.

Though the entire Law was open to strong objections, as judged by the very principles of freedom for which the Republic professed such respect, it was the clause prohibiting the Orders from teaching and suspending their educational activities at such short notice that aroused not only the unanimous opposition of those chiefly concerned but also the protests of many anti-clericals. It was clearly an interference with the liberty of the subject to prevent a man from having his children educated by whom he pleased, especially since the schools of the Orders were confessedly among the most competent in the country.[1] But the sheer ridiculousness of suppressing these schools—especially the Jesuits' schools—at such a time was what shocked moderate opinion most. The views of the educationist and ex-Minister of Education, Don Salvador de Madariaga, one of the first Ambassadors and best friends of the young Republic, who has stringently criticized the Church again and again, may be cited as typical of what many who loved the clergy no

[1] The Church and the Orders, however, were not, as Mr. Henry Brinton (*Christianity and Spain*, p. 17) declares, "almost entirely responsible for education." This inaccurate statement is repeated on p. 27 ("Education was almost exclusively in the hands of the Church"). I know no evidence whatever for the charge that "there was a terribly poor educational system because the Church used its great power to ensure that there should not be one," and I believe this charge to be entirely without foundation.

more than he did were thinking. "The Second Republic," he wrote, "has ruined a magnificent opportunity of directing the problem of secondary education towards a satisfactory solution. Obsessed by its anti-clericalism, it has light-heartedly closed down the only type of school that, for all its imperfection, bore some slight resemblance to a secondary school—the Jesuit college. And having done this it has created more and more State secondary schools—that is to say, spiritless caricatures of universities, branches of Messrs. Textbook and Company, Limited. . . .[1] In matters of secondary education, the Republic has failed dismally."[2]

That was no more than the simple truth, expressed again and again about this time by people from whom one would least expect to hear it. "The Republic is making life absurdly complicated for itself," wrote Sr. Puig y Cadafalch,[3] one of the most enlightened and statesmanlike of Spaniards, "as if there were not already sufficiently difficult and urgent problems for it to solve. How can this country dispense with the services of hundreds of able and disinterested men, who have made teaching their vocation?"

Let us describe the educational situation in the simplest possible terms. When the Republic was launched, about thirty per cent of the population was illiterate.[4] Elementary education, free and in theory compulsory, was not available to hundreds of thousands of children (46,000 in Madrid alone)[5] because there were not sufficient schools for them

[1] The reference is to the custom by which teachers in Spanish State secondary schools produce text-books and market them at a large profit. The author has described this type of school (*op. cit.*, p. 247) as "a caricature of the University and a vast commercial enterprise for the exploitation of text-books."

[2] *Anarquía o Jerarquía*, p. 248.

[3] *Catalonia Infelix*, p. 164.

[4] Not "half the population," as Mr. Brinton (*Christianity and Spain*, p. 27) hazards. The latest statistics available will be found in José Bergua: *Psicología del pueblo español* (Madrid, 1934), pp. 325, 447, n.

[5] *Times Educational Supplement*, June 6, 1931. A census taken about the same time (*El Sol*, June 2, 1931), reports that Madrid had 146 State primary schools ("of which not all are at present functioning"), with classes averaging 57 children each. In these schools, 34,867 children were receiving instruction, while 45,783 children were not being educated at all. Even after five years

to go to. Secondary education, as we have seen, was unsatisfactory, but there was also too little of it. Most large towns, including Barcelona, the largest city in Spain, had only one "Instituto," or State secondary school: Madrid—being the capital—had two.[1]

The Republic was pledged by its principles to improve this state of things. It was indeed high time that something was done: the State had for too long been content to let the Church do its work and save it money. The Ministry of Education began energetically to build schools and to train teachers, both elementary and secondary. No less than 5,300 schools were projected for the first year. In three months, 3,000 of them had been built; and, though progress then became slower, the number had, by the end of 1932, reached 9,600. Yet the total number estimated as necessary was 27,000: it would take several years more to complete this programme and longer still to provide and train teachers efficiently.[2]

And now, within another year, the Government proposed to disband, all over the country, schools giving instruction at least as adequate as that which it was itself providing in increasing quantity and which Sr. de Madariaga described as being, "even after three years of the Republic, detestable."[3] It proposed to turn nearly 350,000 children out of school (this figure was its own: the Catholic Press made it much higher) and to dispense with the services of some 4,500 teachers, all trained or experienced, only a small number

of Republican rule, "there were still 10,000 to 12,000 children in Madrid for whom the elementary schools had no accommodation" (*ibid.*, August 15, 1936). From this last source we learn also that in Barcelona, under the Monarchy, the "State primary schools had room for only 2,000 children."

[1] The Madrid Institutos were Cardenal Cisneros and San Isidro. Not counting about twenty "local" secondary schools in smaller towns, there were, before 1931, seventy-two Institutos in Spain, with one master for each subject taught; Geography and History were counted as one subject, as were Physics and Chemistry. There were also twenty Schools of Commerce in Spain. This and other information on education under the Monarchy will be found in the *Guía Oficial de España* for 1929.

[2] *The Spanish Tragedy*, p. 126; *Times Educational Supplement*, August 15, 1936.

[3] *Anarquía o Jerarquía*, p. 220. Cf. *The Spanish Tragedy*, p. 124.

of whom it would incorporate into its own schools. In Madrid, to take a particular example, there were 78 schools kept by religious communities with a total of 25,500 pupils. The result of this legislation would be to throw almost as many children upon the streets as were there under the Monarchy, to undo the work of the Republic and to post-pone for at least a further two years the absorption of all the children in the city. In the province of Barcelona, the Orders maintained 340 schools educating 41,100 pupils. Few provinces had less than a thousand children in such schools, and in Murcia and Alicante, two of the provinces in which illiteracy is highest, there were as many as 10,500.

It was obvious that to close efficient schools of any kind at such a time was mere foolishness, dictated by intolerance, which is always blind. Confronted with these figures, the Government, with that invincible light-heartedness which thrives so well in Spain, chose to minimize the obstacles which it had created for itself. Only 7,000 more schools would be needed for complete absorption, declared the Minister of Education, and half of these were already provided for. There was ample time and money to "create" the rest. ("Create" was a good word! Creation is not so difficult a task when it can be partly done by confiscation.) Buildings, no doubt, could be found not a hundred yards from the schools that were to be closed, but how would lay teachers for 250,000 children—and teachers who could be trusted to instil into their instruction the ideas favoured by the Government—be formed and trained between June 1933, when the Law was promulgated, and the following December, when the elementary schools of the Orders were to close? Fortunately, the situation never arose, as the Government fell and fresh elections were held in November, as a result of which, over a period of two years, the schools of the Orders were allowed to continue indefinitely.

Just upon one hundred more deputies voted for the

Law of Congregations than had voted for the twenty-sixth Article of the Constitution. The President of the Republic, however, hesitated a good deal longer about signing it than he had before signing the Constitution. It was not, indeed, until the very last day of grace allowed him by the Constitution that he did so. He certainly could not plead ignorance of the opinion of the country, which was to be shown by so dramatic a turn-over of votes in six months' time. Petitions and protests in enormous volume arrived at the Presidential Palace; those able to do so approached the President privately; the Metropolitan Bishops issued a collective letter summarizing the recent anti-clerical laws and provocative actions of the Government. On the day after the promulgation of the Law, a papal Encyclical, *Dilectissima Nobis*, expressed the opinion of the Vatican.

So the Law was added to the statute-book and the teaching Orders prepared to make one more sacrifice on the altar of intolerance. By this time the nation was fully awake to the campaign of persecution which had begun. It was not merely a question of laws and decrees affecting the whole country. There were quiet and insidious attempts, such as never get into the papers, to remove practising Catholics from their employments and offices. There were municipal orders and restrictions of which little was heard and which sound of little importance when one refers to them individually, but which aimed at uprooting the age-long customs of devotion so dear to Spaniards and of implanting in their place a neo-paganism which the huge majority of them will never accept.

In the spring of 1933, during a long tour which covered the four quarters of the Peninsula, I had occasion to note how the now open hostility of a relatively small number of people who had formerly professed orthodoxy was strengthening, not weakening, the faith of the people. Everywhere there was vigorous life, constant hope and unabated courage. At Seville, in the preceding year, the Church's enemies had been so violent that only one courageous confraternity had ventured out in the Holy Week procession, with the result that revolver shots were fired at it and there was almost tragedy. So this year no processions went out at all; the hotels were empty of tourists; and, despite temperatures of eighty degrees in the shade, the city had quite lost its animation. Yet Seville was more strikingly devout than I had ever seen it before. The number of church services was increased; the *pasos*, ablaze with lights and surrounded with banks of flowers, were placed in the churches of their confraternities; and thus the non-emergence of the Church into the streets had the result of drawing thousands from the streets into the churches.

The change, in short, was bad for trade but good for religion. Similar evidence was obtainable from Madrid, where I arrived on the morning of Good Friday. It might have been the morning of a popular festival—indeed, it was, for Good Friday that year coincided with the second birthday of the Republic. There was bunting at all the windows of Government buildings and Republican flags were mast-high everywhere. Yet Good Friday was observed in Madrid (and *a fortiori* elsewhere in Spain) with all its traditional solemnity. No doubt the Government thought it was pleasing the people when it cancelled the ban set by a previous *régime* on the opening of theatres and cinemas on Maundy Thursday and Good Friday. The result in Madrid was simply this. Of its twenty theatres and thirty-six cinemas, only one theatre and ten cinemas opened; and of these ten, five showed only films on sacred subjects. The Constitution of 1931 might declare that Spain had no official religion; the people of Spain responded by showing how far removed was that statement from reality.

They gave, in fact, ample proof that they were as religious a people as ever. Throughout the country, shops and offices still closed on the afternoons of the great festivals, despite the official abolition of these holy days as holidays. I had never seen larger or more devout congregations than on St. Joseph's Day in Barcelona Cathedral or for the great *Hora Santa*, which is observed in Valencia Cathedral on the Thursday in Passion Week. Indeed, in this respect it was difficult to see any marked difference between the Spain of 1933 and of 1930. It takes more than the running-up of flags to full-mast on Good Friday to change a nation's religion.

One striking illustration of the soundness of Spain's Catholicity is of particular interest. The Basques are, as most people now know, among the staunchest Catholics in the country and in no region of Spain during these years were the continual attempts that went on to undermine their customs more strongly resisted. In the largest of the Basque cities, Bilbao, the Municipal Council had resolved, by a majority of three, to remove from its place in a public square a large monument to the Sacred Heart which was a great centre of popular devotion. The women of Bilbao protested strongly. For weeks, by night and by day, they came in groups to make acts of reparation and testify their devotion to Our Lord until the Civil Governor issued an order that they were not to be allowed to remain in the vicinity of the monument, "still less to pray there." Even then, so many women persisted in disobeying the order that shock troops had to be employed to remove them.

Some two years after these incidents, in the book already referred to, Don Salvador de Madariaga confirmed the estimate here made in a striking condemnation of the attitude of Sr. Azaña's Governments to religion. "The gravest error of the Republic of the 14th of April was its religious policy. . . . The decatholicization of Spain has been almost *nil* as far as women are concerned, and as regards men it has been only slight and superficial. For a long time, therefore, Spain will continue to be a Catholic nation, perhaps the most Catholic nation in the world."[1]

The biennium during which the Centre and Centre-Right were in power (November 1933–February 1936) was far less troubled than the five months which followed it but was certainly not a period on which Spain could look back with satisfaction. Stagnation, irresolution and continual changes of government were the order of the day and there was little real progress.[2] Had the Right been permitted by the President to form a Government, the story might have been a different one. But even then little could have been done while the Government was encumbered by the millstone of a Socialistic Constitution. According to the final article of this it could not be revised during the first four years except by the vote of at least two-thirds of the deputies in the Cortes—that is to say, of about 310—a figure unlikely to be reached. It is true that in the new Cortes there were 374 Centre and Right deputies to only 99 of the Left, but by no means all the Centre deputies—largely belonging to the Radical party, whose leaders had been in the Cabinet of the Constituent Cortes—could be relied upon to vote with the Right. In practice, therefore, a right-wing Government would have had to wait until the end of 1935 before proposing a reform of the Constitution, after which date an absolute majority in the Cortes would suffice for the revision of any one article.

The wrongs done to the Church, then, during the past two and a half years could not be immediately or permanently righted. All that the successive Governments could do, despite their huge majority in the Cortes, was to defer or modify the operation of the anti-clerical measures

---

[1] *Anarquía o Jerarquía*, p. 218. [2] *The Spanish Tragedy*, pp. 141–89.

of the Left Governments. This they at once did. A law
assured to clergy who in April 1931 had been beneficed
priests two-thirds of their salaries for the current year.
The substitution of lay schools for religious was postponed
indefinitely. Negotiations with the Holy See, which had
been broken during the previous biennium, were resumed,
and a temporary arrangement was made by which the
Foreign Minister went to the Vatican as "Ambassador
Extraordinary."

The two years, then, passed quietly for the Church, save
for the destruction which occurred on each of the occasions
when Anarcho-Syndicalists or Communists made abortive
attempts to bring about the proletarian revolution: the
deliberate church-burnings at Granada and Calatayud in
December 1933 and the wrecking of churches and cathedral
at Oviedo in October 1934. Towards the summer of 1935,
the Centre-Right Government and its supporters began to
think seriously of the possibility of a reform of the Constitution in the near future. At any time after December 8
of that year, an absolute majority alone in the Cortes
would be required and that that could be obtained with
ease there was no doubt. The 1931 Constitution had been
drawn up under the influence of strong antipathy to tradition and in June the Government of the day issued a
memorandum summarizing its proposals for reform to be
submitted to the Cortes during the winter: these, needless
to say, included a drastic rehandling of Articles 26 and 27,
held to stand in need of revision even on "strictly political"
grounds, and also of Article 43, on marriage and divorce,
which is described as having exercised an unsatisfactory
influence on the family. It was while these proposals were
in the air that Sr. de Madariaga published the book already
mentioned in which he condemns the religious policy of
Sr. Azaña's Governments. "The Republic," he urged,
"must approach the religious question without prejudices

157

either for or against the Catholic Church, its dogma and its faith, with its mind fixed only upon realities. The omnipresence of Catholicism in Spain is evident and the depth to which it is rooted is proverbial."[1] This outspoken book, coming from an author of such notably left-wing tendencies, caused a deep impression, and would undoubtedly have had an important influence on the debates had a revision of the Constitution been attempted. But at the beginning of the year 1936, the President of the Republic dissolved the Cortes and appointed February 16 for new elections. On the result of those elections would depend, among other things, the fate of the Constitution.

Everybody knows what happened in February 1936. The Popular Front—a coalition of Republican parties of the Left with Socialists, Syndicalists, Anarchists, Unified Marxists and Communists—won the day, with a small but workable majority. Then history repeated itself. Seeing that the reaction had swung, however slightly, in their favour, the extremists of the Left began to riot. General strikes were declared all over the country; prisons were attacked and political prisoners set free; land, especially in the south, was forcibly seized by peasants; assassinations and riots, in which many were killed or wounded, became frequent. But the most characteristic note of those five months following the elections was the passion that was unleashed against the Church. As a hundred years earlier, stories were invented and believed freely. This time it was not monks who had poisoned wells; it was nuns who had given poisoned sweets to children. Later, when War broke out, it was to be priests firing on the "people" from church windows or distributing poisoned tobacco in the trenches. Any story was good—or bad—enough (indeed, to many no story was necessary) to excuse the wholesale burning of

[1] *Anarquía o Jerarquía*, p. 218.

158

churches and religious houses.[1] In the first four months of that period no less than 170 of such buildings were set on fire and attempts were made to burn 251 more: these were figures quoted in the Cortes and not disputed. The destruction was not confined to a restricted area. Two of Madrid's churches—San Ignacio and San Luis—were burned down; and from Logroño, in the north, in which two churches and four monasteries or convents were destroyed, to Elche, in the south-east, which lost three churches, the incendiarism was distributed over nearly the whole country.

Three features of this incendiarism deserve notice. First, its extent. When on the outbreak of the War it was reproduced on an immensely larger scale, those who supported the side responsible for it urged in extenuation that churches had been used by the enemy and sometimes even that priests and monks had taken arms against them.[2] But no such reasons can be alleged in explanation of the church-burning which took place *before the War began*, nor, having regard to the wide field of its operations, could it be described as the

[1] It is hardly necessary to give serious consideration to the charge that, at the beginning of the Civil War, churches were used as fortresses and priests fired on the "people" and that this explains the burning of churches everywhere in Republican territory. The story is probably in part a propagandist fabrication and in part arises from the fact that churches and religious houses, like schools, offices and other kinds of building, were occupied by whichever side could capture them. It is examined in detail and properly disposed of by Carreras, pp. 27–38. Those who desire left-wing testimony on the matter of church-burnings may be referred to George Orwell (*New English Weekly*, November 24, 1938, p. 105): "Churches have been destroyed all over Government Spain. Various Government partisans, in their efforts to make their cause respectable, have pretended that churches were only demolished when they had been used as fortresses in the street fighting at the beginning of the War. This is merely a lie."

[2] Sr. Moreno, a whole-hearted supporter of the Popular Front, asserts (*op. cit.*, pp. 32–3) that in Madrid, on July 20, 1936, he "saw the militia being fired on from the windows of the Church of Our Lady of Covadonga," and on the following day "saw signs of the previous day's fighting in the Cathedral, in San Andrés and in the convent of Santa Isabel la Real. This," he adds, "may explain the violence which broke out in Madrid and caused the burning of fourteen churches. But there is no possible justification for that used in other places, where the aggression came from the multitude, giving rise to abominable scenes in which the only thing that shines forth clearly is the dignity with which Bishops, nuns and priests accepted their martyr's crown." These and similar accusations are shown in their true light by Carreras, pp. 27–38.

work of a few irresponsible eccentrics. The only excuse for it which I have heard given is that, in some churches (unspecified), certain priests (unnamed) had on various occasions exhorted their congregations to vote against the Popular Front. Such vague accusations are impossible of investigation.[1] To judge from Cardinal Gomá's strictures on party politics[2] and the attitude taken throughout these years by the hierarchy, they would seem highly improbable. Still there are many parish priests in Spain and it is conceivable that here and there a priest may have preached politics. But assuming that to be so, it can hardly be thought surprising if congregations were advised to vote against a coalition consisting of one group of parties which had been largely responsible for the continuous attacks on the Church during the Red Biennium and another group which was professedly and openly anti-Christian. One would hardly expect them to have been exhorted to support anti-Christian legislation. In any case, it is not usual in a civilized country, if in a church or chapel the congregation is advised to support one side or the other in an election, for the church or chapel to be burned down in reprisal. However, constant reading of the left-wing Press having failed to produce a single accusation of this kind giving place and name, let alone date, it must be considered doubtful that any preacher did more than point out the responsibility which would rest with the electors should further anti-Christian legislation be passed as a result of the polling.

The second feature of these church-burnings is that they were freely, if not universally, attributed to the Anarchists—not so much by the Right as by many politicians and supporters of the Left who sincerely deplored them—which, of course, a large majority did. And, as has already been shown, the Anarchist creed is founded, not upon

[1] The nearest approach which I have seen to a specific charge, though not precisely of the kind mentioned, will be found in Semprún Gurrea, p. 18.
[2] Cf. p. 142, above.

mere anti-clericalism, but upon denial of the existence of God.

Thirdly, what did the Government do, and what did the people do, in face of these repeated attacks on Church property? The people did nothing: what could they have done? The peace of a village or small town is disturbed without warning one fine day by a lorry which stops outside a church or monastery and from which emerges a band of armed men who proceed to soak the building with cans of petrol and set light to it. What precisely does one do in such circumstances? Call the village policeman? In the larger towns, above all in Madrid, there were more than sufficient Civil Guards and police to stop the attacks had the Government so desired. After the War had begun, the Popular Front's supporters complained, not without reason, that they could hardly be expected to check disorder and violence when the greater proportion of the forces of law and order had revolted against them. But this plea could not be made to account for the impunity which rewarded the earlier activities of the incendiaries. The protest made by the Holy See in August would have come even more appropriately in June:

> Admitting that the Madrid Government may often find considerable difficulties in checking such deplorable excesses . . . nevertheless, we cannot forget that, as in the past, the insistent and repeated demands of the Holy See have not succeeded in bringing the Government to intervene effectively in order to check and punish violence against the Church. Satisfaction has not up to the present been afforded to the just remonstrances of the Holy See.
>
> All men of good will expect some intervention on the part of the Madrid Government so that these lamentable excesses may be quelled, or, at least, that the Government should publicly express its regret at these sacrilegious

acts, openly and distinctly disassociating itself from the responsibility attaching to the authors of the crimes[1]

Nothing of the sort happened. For five months, disorder and destruction, with many other excesses, were allowed by a responsible Government to continue unchecked. "Have the profoundest respect for authority," Cardinal Gomá had written; "it is the guarantee of social order."[2] The words sound ironic when we think of the Popular Front Government. Whatever one's view of armed rebellion in principle and of the subsequent action of the Spanish Army in particular, one cannot be surprised that a revolt should break out against a Government which had tolerated (and by its attitude encouraged) such outrages. The Popular Front was only reaping, more quickly than it might have expected, where it had sown.

[1] *The Tablet*, August 15, 1936.
[2] Gomá, I, 277. ("Horas graves.")

CHAPTER VI

THE ORDERS AND THE CIVIL WAR

ONE OF the essential facts to bear in mind about the Civil War—a fact about which there can be no dispute —is that the revolt of the Right, where it failed to establish itself, was immediately followed by a counter-revolt of the extreme Left—by that "proletarian revolution," in fact, for which, to its organizers, the Republic had been nothing but a preparation, and which, during the Republic's five years' life, they had made several attempts to establish.[1] Any doubt as to this would be immediately dispelled by a glance at the sub-titles of leading newspapers in Barcelona and Valencia—*Diario de la Revolución*—or at the exhortations painted along the sides of railway coaches—"For the Revolution, work!" Some of the extremists went so far as to put the Revolution in importance before the War; and if to others the War was more important than the Revolution the reason was only that the Revolution could not be fully consummated until the War was won. Whether we blame or applaud the Army for revolting against the Government of February–July 1936—and many even of those who realize the Government's criminal incompetence think that the Generals acted precipitately—we cannot deny that on Popular Front territory that revolution at once came into being.

In one sense all the parties composing the Popular Front are responsible for the outbreak of this revolution and for the excesses committed in its name; but the primary responsibility must rest with the groups which had openly announced its advent and had endeavoured to bring it in earlier—the Anarchists, the Syndicalists and (with some degree of

---

[1] Cf. *The Spanish Tragedy*, pp. 90–1, 121, 128, 144, 168–73, where five of these attempts are described in detail.

collaboration on the part of left-wing Socialists) the Communists. It is true that Sr. Peiró, an Anarchist leader, claims that those whom he would group as "bourgeois Republicans" were equally responsible for the excesses, and no doubt in the exaltation of the first few days of the Revolution crimes were committed by individuals belonging to the moderate Republican parties or to the Catalan Esquerra.[1] But against this must be set the discovery of such documents as those officially issued at Gijón in October 1936 by the Anarcho-Syndicalists, and bearing the words: "The holder of this safe-conduct is to be used for no other work than the destruction of churches, on which he is now employed."[2] All evidence goes to show that the large majority of the excesses were the work of Anarcho-Syndicalists and Communists, and were carried out by order of responsible committees of these bodies, acting on pre-arranged lines. The point is of importance, as we shall see later.

The full story of the martyrdom of the Church in Spain during the early months of the Civil War has not yet been told nor will it be told until evidence can be collected, examined and sifted with due care. Quite conceivably such a process will show some of the reports to have been exaggerated, and persons believed to be dead, as has already happened on both sides, may reappear safe and sound. But it is to be feared that a far larger number of crimes of which nothing is at present known will be discovered and that persons believed to be alive will be found to have perished. Details given below have, as far as is possible, been checked—some of them by the responsible heads of the religious Orders concerned—but no suggestion is made that this is anything more than a tentative and an interim report, the chief object of which is to contrast the attacks made on the Orders in 1936–7 with earlier attacks, both as to facts and as to motives.

[1] *Catalonia Infelix*, p. 252, n. 6. [2] Carreras, p. 41. Cf. also p. 115.

For this reason I do not attempt to describe in any detail the terrible scenes which took place on the outbreak of the Revolution and which have been described fully elsewhere: the sack or destruction of churches (estimated by the Spanish Bishops at about 20,000[1]) and the loss of countless and irreplaceable art treasures of every description; the wholesale murder, over a period of months, of priests, religious, seminarists, choir-boys and devout lay people of every description; the tortures to which many of these were subjected and the inhuman ways in which they were killed; the frightful profanations, not merely of Church buildings and furniture, of relics and other objects of veneration, and of the Reserved Sacrament, but even of the bodies of persons recently murdered and of others long since dead— and one had believed that in every civilized country, and in all circumstances, the dead, whatever they might have done when living, were treated with the greatest possible respect. If, for a moment, I dwell on these murders and atrocities, the huge majority of them entirely unprovoked— for the Church, as we have seen, had taken no side in the quarrel between Right and Left, and many of the murdered must have been supporters of the Popular Front—it is to express a wonder, which as yet has hardly been given adequate expression, that the performance of such deeds could have aroused so little comment.

An earthquake claims a thousand victims and the entire world thrills with sympathy. A mine disaster throws a village into mourning and subscriptions and messages of condolence pour in from rich and poor. A cat or a dog is tortured, and the news, featured by every paper in the land, is received with just indignation. In our own country the assassination of a single clergyman and the hunt for his murderers would be front-page news for many days on end. The murder of a politically minded Dean or Bishop on the

---

[1] *Joint Letter*, p. 17.

eve of a general election would not only stir the entire nation but might easily lose the election for the party which had not enjoyed his sympathies. And yet, in the course of a few weeks, ten Spanish Bishops, something like six thousand secular priests and a total of about sixteen thousand priests, monks, nuns and lay workers were murdered in cold blood: "many had their limbs amputated or were terribly mutilated before being put to death; their eyes were gouged out or their tongues cut out; they were ripped open, burned or buried alive, hewn to death with axes."[1] And we receive the news with complete equanimity. To some extent this may at first have been due to doubts as to its accuracy or to the overshadowing of the Anarcho-Communist Revolution by the Civil War. But any such doubts have long ceased to exist and still this Christian nation is unmoved.

It is little more than two years since these thousands of our fellow Christians were tortured and killed—and our attitude to their sufferings is as remote as to those of the victims of the Emperor Nero. For over two years, in the Spain ruled by the Popular Front, Catholics have been forbidden to meet freely in their churches for public worship —and we Englishmen, who in the past have said so much about freedom of worship, treat the matter as entirely normal. Surely Christian people, who put Christianity before politics, should long ago have made up their minds on one thing. They may not support General Franco or desire to see a totalitarian *régime* in Spain—that is a perfectly understandable position—but at least they will not, either by word or act, support the side which has abolished religious liberty and whose supporters have been responsible for crimes to which in modern history it would be difficult to find a parallel.

Let us now try to obtain some idea as to the losses suffered

[1] *Joint Letter*, p. 18.

by the religious Orders during the proletarian revolution. So numerous are they that it is impossible to refer to more than a few. I will first describe some of the lists of martyrs in my possession which have been drawn up by the provincial officers of Orders with which I have been in close touch for many years and afterwards cite other kinds of testimony. The first list relates to the Catalonian Province of the Capuchin Fathers and covers the first eleven months of the War. It gives the name and age of each victim; the community to which he had belonged; the date, where this is known, of his assassination; the place where it occurred; and in some cases, particulars of the murder. The total number of victims, including six as to whose fate there is not yet complete certainty, is thirty-seven. Of these, twenty-one were priests, eleven of them over fifty; seven were theological students of between eighteen and twenty-three; and nine were lay brothers whose average age was exactly fifty. They lived in nine different communities and met their deaths in places as unlike as the Catalonian capital, the cathedral city of Lérida, the country town of Olot, the seaside resort of Canet and the country village of Palautordera. Six of the Fathers were members of the community of Sarrià, near Barcelona. I knew them well; they were great students, frequent contributors to *Estudis Franciscans*; and one or another of them, conspicuous by his brown habit and long beard, was generally to be seen in the library of the Institute of Catalan Studies. They had also an excellent library of their own, where I often visited them and discussed matters of common interest. When not in their library, one saw them most frequently in their large garden; I never knew a more lovable community or one living so near a large city which seemed so far removed from things of the world. Of the six martyrs, the youngest was P. Agustí de Montclar, something of a poet, who had distinguished himself by a contribution to a recent volume of homage to the memory of Ramón Lull. Another of the younger scholars was P. Doroteu de Vilalba, whom I was just getting to know by his articles but had never met. The most remarkable of the group was P. Martí de Barcelona, a rather older man of quite formidable erudition but so approachable that he was everybody's friend and helper. But my greatest friend at Sarrià was one of the oldest of the friars, P. Vicente Peralta. Sixty-four years of age, the list says: I had always thought him to be more. He had made a life-long study of the Spanish mystics and they seemed to have infused into him something of their other-worldliness and tranquillity. I have the details of his death but I would rather not give them. They tortured him first. . . .

The Escolapians—a teaching Order often specifically exempted from anti-clerical persecutions in the nineteenth century—have lost, according to the latest official report, 110 of their 1,475 brethren; two of these were burned alive at Peralta de la Sal, in Aragon. Learning, as well as religion, has suffered by their deaths: P. Enrique Ejarque, shot in the cemetery at Castellón, was a notable authority on pedagogical theory; P. Alberto Bertomeu, murdered in Barcelona, had published a great deal of work on experimental psychology; P. José Cerdeiriña and P. Luciano Menesalvas, of Madrid, were also well known for their scholarly publications. Except in their Basque province, the Escolapians lost practically the whole of their colleges, churches and libraries. Their Colegio de San Fernando, in Madrid, with a library rich in *incunabula* and another used widely by specialists in Biblical studies, was completely destroyed. In Valencia, the seventeenth-century Colegio Andresiano was burned to the ground, with its church, library and museum. At Barcelona, the Colegio de San Antón (which with its thirteenth-century chapel had been destroyed during the Tragic Week of 1909 and afterwards rebuilt) was burned down, and the greatly venerated house of San José de Calasanz, at Peralta de la Sal, was profaned and destroyed.

So one might go on. While a full martyrology will take years to compile, the interim reports, of which I have copies dated May 1938, are sufficiently revelatory. The Claretians, one of the more recent Orders, seem to have suffered the most severely; their martyrs total to date 237. In all their provinces—Andalusia, Aragon, Castile, Catalonia and Valencia—they have had grievous losses. At Madrid, their death-roll of twenty-one included three priests seventy-five years old. At Ciudad Real, fourteen of their students were murdered. At Barbastro, in Aragon, the Claretian college was assaulted, and no less than fifteen teachers and thirty-three students were slaughtered. In one of the two Barcelona houses, ten were killed; in the other, seven, five of these being men of sixty. At Cervera, where one hundred and fifty brethren occupied the buildings of the abandoned nineteenth-century university, they were invaded on July 20, 1936, and given one hour in which to escape. Fifty-six are known to have been killed, twenty-one of them young students; some of these were tortured before being killed, in a vain attempt to make them renounce their faith.[1] The fate of one group which attempted to escape is particularly tragic. The novice-master, P. Jover, took charge of a party of fourteen novices who, like himself, had relatives at a hamlet called, in Catalan, Vallbona de les Monges, not far from Borjas Blancas, near Lérida. They arrived safely; but some militiamen quartered there determined to kill them. So, despite attempts made by their friends to save them, they murdered them then and there, pursuing into the country those who succeeded in escaping. The novice-master was shot in the presence of his own father.[2]

[1] They were forced to swallow medals and rosaries and rosary-beads were thrust into their ears. (Carreras, p. 147.)
[2] *La Persécution religieuse*, etc., pp. 108-9.

Another teaching Order, the Brothers of the Christian Schools, had 148 martyrs, including many of the teaching Brothers, and also chaplains, novice-masters and several of the headmasters of the schools for the poor. Of the older Orders, the Franciscans lost 104;[1] the Dominicans, after tracing the murders of 52, have many of their Fathers still unaccounted for. In this way one might go down the list of the twenty-eight Orders which so far have sent in their death-rolls; there are still more to come.[2]

Another source of evidence than the lists drawn up by the Orders is a book entitled *La Persécution religieuse en Espagne*. Like much other material of the kind, it had to be published anonymously, the author's relatives being at the time still in Popular Front Spain. I am now allowed to say that it was written by Dr. Juan Estelrich, a distinguished Catalonian man of letters, who since 1931 has been a member of the Spanish Republican Parliament and for some time held office in the Catalan Government. I know personally of the care with which his statistics have been collected; some of them I have checked by other testimony; and the names and minor details which for the reader's convenience are omitted here will all be found in the original or in the author's own files.

In describing the losses suffered by the Orders, Sr. Estelrich limits himself, for reasons of space, to the part of Spain with which he is most familiar. He takes, first, the Monastery of Montserrat, to which reference has already been made. It houses the largest Benedictine community in Spain and

---

[1] Seven Franciscans from Azuaga, in the province of Badajoz, had their tongues cut out and their ears severed while still alive. (Carreras, p. 147.)

[2] I have also lists of the martyred secular clergy (some of them used by Bayle, pp. 76–82), the longest and fullest of which relates to the Archdiocese of Toledo. In this, 176 priests are known to have been murdered. The Dean of Toledo Cathedral had his tongue cut out before being shot; D. Mariano Gómez Cediel, a priest of over sixty, was shot in the legs before being despatched; D. Tomás Galindo Romero, of Mocejón, was mutilated while still alive. As to the murders of clergy, choirmen, servers, organists, and parish priests from Toledo itself, the account will seem incredible when published in full and cannot fail to shock world opinion.

is situated in the heart of the country, far from any theatre of war or possible centre of conspiracy. At the very beginning of the Revolution, an attempt made to destroy the monastery was, by a lucky chance,[1] frustrated. On July 22 four lorry-loads of Anarcho-Syndicalists, with their usual incendiary equipment, drew up outside the buildings. One of the men, however, happened to see a workmate who was staying there with his mother; and the mother, overhearing the intentions of the gang, engaged some of them in conversation. She pointed out to them that the monastery and its shrine were something more than an ordinary church, and that the Moreneta ("Black Virgin"), which is venerated there, was one of the historic possessions of Catalonia. Her arguments had some effect; and, while the men were discussing what to do, a member of the Catalan parliament arrived on the scene, accompanied by a squad of armed police, with orders to take over the monastery for the Government. This was done, and its inmates were allowed to leave it. But, though some of them were able to embark safely for Italy, thirty are known to have been killed.[2] Of those who took refuge in private houses in Barcelona, seven were assassinated: P. José María Fontseré, an old monk of eighty-two; P. Domingo González, aged fifty-two; P. Juan Roca, aged fifty-six, an eminent authority on music and a personal friend of Millet and Casals; P. Ambrosio Busquets, a specialist in patristics, who had translated St. Bernard and was preparing a critical edition of a work by St. Basil; P. Plácido Feliu, Head of Montserrat's famous choir-school; and two lay brothers, one of whom worked in the Montserrat printing-press and one in the bindery. These, with a few others, had left their temporary lodgings and taken up residence together in a flat which was used by members

[1] Described in Carreras, pp. 182–4.
[2] Carreras (p. 184), writing later than Estelrich, makes the total over forty. My own list, giving the names and ages of the victims and particulars of their deaths, is nearer the lower total than the higher.

of the community who might be passing through Barcelona. At eleven o'clock on the night of August 19, 1936, a band of militiamen forcibly entered the premises, seized these seven religious and bundled them into two cars: after their execution, their bodies were taken to the Clinical Hospital and then given burial. Two more Fathers were assassinated at a later date in Barcelona—P. Luis Palacios, the author of a Syriac and an Aramaic grammar who had been a professor of Oriental Languages in Jerusalem and Rome and P. Veremundo Bocquer, a younger scholar, newly appointed Archivist at Montserrat in succession to P. Albareda.[1]

Among the other Montserrat martyrs was a second authority on music, P. Ángel Rodamilans, who had joined his family at Sabadell. It was a natural, but an unfortunate move, for he was recognized by some revolutionaries and taken off without notice to a firing-squad. Ordered to renounce his faith, he replied by a triumphant reiteration of it, whereupon he was shot.[2]

Three more Fathers were shot at Molíns de Rey, two at Tarragona, one at Vich, one at Gélida and four at Pedralbes: these last were imprisoned for some weeks previously in the Model Prison at Barcelona.

The Jesuits suffered less severely than would have been the case had they still existed as a Society, but more than forty of them, who had been taking advantage of the permission given them to live in Spain as individuals, were murdered, including P. Bori, superintendent of a leper hospital, who had fled to Valencia but was tracked down and killed there.[3] Down to the spring of 1937, twenty-seven had lost their lives in the Province of Aragon, eight in the Province of Toledo and seven and five respectively in the Provinces of León and Andalusia.

P. Braulio Martínez, shot at Tarragona, was eighty-five

[1] Cf. p. 108, above.   [2] *La Persécution religieuse* ,etc., pp. 97–9.
Carreras, p. 136.

years of age and for more than thirty years had been
Professor of Canon Law at a Tarragona seminary. But he
was also a prison chaplain, known far and wide for his life
of voluntary poverty and self-sacrifice. He had on occasion
given to poor people the very clothes he was wearing and
there was a saying that no one had ever seen him in a new
cassock.[1] Yet even such as he were needed to feed the
flames of anti-Christian passion.

A striking description of the martyrdom of two Jesuit
priests and a lay brother comes from an eye-witness, P. José
María Murall, who had been Provincial of the Society's
Aragonese province and at the time of the outbreak of
war was living with three other priests and a lay brother at
a retreat house in Barcelona.[2] Upon the first disturbances
they separated, but on the morning of July 21, 1936, while
two priests of the Society were visiting P. Murall and the
lay brother who had remained with him, seven armed men
entered, ordered them to don lay attire and to board two cars
bearing the letters C.N.T. and F.A.I.[3] which were in waiting.
They had no difficulty in guessing what was going to happen.

The cars stopped at the headquarters of a Syndicate and
were surrounded by revolutionaries. "You are priests,"
they cried, "and we are going to kill you. Not one of you
shall escape."

After a few minutes' wait, the cars went on into the
country, and, at a lonely spot near a hillside, the four men
were taken out, lined up and shot. Two were killed outright; a third was finished off by the murderers as he lay
on the grass in agony. P. Murall, though so gravely
wounded that he was taken for dead, remained conscious
and was picked up by a passing car and taken to a hospital.
In some way his escape appears to have become known, for
on several occasions Anarchists presented themselves at the

[1] *La Persécution religieuse*, etc., pp. 103–4. [2] *Op. cit.*, pp. 168–72.
[3] The initials of the Syndicalist and Anarchist Unions respectively.

hospital and demanded that he should be surrendered to them. The doctor in charge, however, succeeded in persuading them that he had been discharged, and after two months he was able to get a boat to Marseilles.

Another series of tragic narratives, supplementing the official lists quoted above, concerns the Orders devoted to education—Salesians, Escolapians, Brothers of the Christian Schools and Marists—and those most saintly men of whose work even an anti-clerical Cabinet Minister could speak with the deepest respect, the Brethren of St. John of God. These were forcibly evicted from the hospitals, asylums and orphan-homes where they were doing so great a work; most of them were imprisoned; some were tortured; many were killed.[1] In particular may be cited the murder of seven of the Brothers in the Málaga sanatorium where they were working; of seven others, Colombians by nationality, assassinated in Barcelona on August 8, 1936, while carrying their passports and wearing badges in their national colours stamped by their legation; and of twenty-two who worked at Calafell, in a hospital for scrofulous children, which was so highly esteemed in Catalonia that public collections for it were periodically sanctioned by the authorities. These last brothers were paraded in lorries round the streets of Vendrell before being executed.[2]

The Marists have lost nearly the whole of their Catalonian schools, and their death-roll, to date, stands at 109. In October 1936, about ninety of these were shot outright, without being given the option of a hearing by the Popular Tribunals, as, with over one hundred of their fellows, they were on the point of embarking on the *Cabo San Antonio* in Barcelona harbour.[3] It was at about the same time that the persecution of another group of two hundred and thirty

[1] *Op. cit.*, pp. 105–6.   [2] Carreras, pp. 132, 134.
[3] *La Persécution religieuse*, etc., pp. 106–7; Carreras, pp. 133–4. There is a slight discrepancy in the figures given by these two authors.

came to a head. These lived in the country, nine miles from the town of Balaguer and so far from civilization that no word of the Revolution reached them till three days after it had begun. Ten days later, a group of Anarchists gave them eight hours to evacuate their house, forbidding any single one of them, even though sick or infirm, to remain. They sought refuge in neighbouring villages; some of them even in the hills and woods. A few dug trenches for themselves, hoping to be safer there. Some of them were hunted and shot; others died of exposure; what happened to the rest none knows. But when, late in September, attempts were made to assemble the community for transference to France, only 108 of the 230 could be found. These, after all their worldly goods but the clothes they wore—even to their medals and crucifixes—had been taken from them, were allowed, with the exception of fifteen, who were detained, to cross the frontier. The fate of the fifteen is at present unknown.[1]

During the anti-clerical persecutions of the nineteenth century, the persons of nuns (though not always their homes and their possessions) were generally respected. Not so in the anti-Christian persecutions of the twentieth century.

Málaga alone has reported the murder of six nuns—Sor Carmen, a Clarissan; Sor María Josefa, a Capuchin; Madre Jesús María y José and Madre Purificación, Franciscans; Sor María de la Santísima Trinidad and Sor Trinidad de San José, Dominicans.

One of the largest and most central convents to be invaded in Barcelona was the Convent of the Good Shepherd, situated in the Gran Vía Diagonal. Here fifty nuns had charge of a home for intractable girls of between fifteen and twenty, of whom between three and four hundred were living there. Militiamen invaded the home; imprisoned the

[1] *Op. cit.*, pp. 107-8.

nuns in a wing of it; and, seizing all the food and drink they could lay their hands on, began a night's orgy. Reinforced by comrades, they repeated their exploit on several nights following. The parents of some of the girls made vain efforts to rescue them, and when at last the men were evicted it was found that many girls were missing.[1]

The road to La Rabassada, the scene of P. Murall's narrative, witnessed also many more gruesome and equally tragic ones, not all of which have as yet been related. On this road, five Dominican nuns from the Annunciata Convent in Barcelona were found to have been violated and shot. Four were already dead; one, who died in hospital on the following day, lived long enough to tell their story. Some months before the Revolution they had come from Montserrat to Barcelona. A band of militiamen had invaded the school where they were living and demanded that any nuns should be surrendered. A woman accused of belonging to the community was so fearful of the consequences of their visit that she betrayed the five nuns. The rest followed quickly.[2]

I have purposely related these details of the persecution of the Orders with all possible brevity: many more horrible accounts have appeared in the sensational Press. My aim has been to show the kind of thing that happened during those months, not to soldiers, to political conspirators or to a few particularly unfortunate persons here and there, but to thousands of harmless priests and laymen, monks and nuns, old men, old women and even children. The crimes described are typical of a much larger number which Christians who support the Popular Front Government have to explain or condone. One may be glad that they have led some Christians at least, who care nothing about party politics, to say: "The cause of men like these can never be mine."

[1] *Op. cit.*, p. 110.
[2] *Op. cit.*, pp. 110–11. Cf. (from another source) *Catalonia Infelix*, p. 260.

CHAPTER VII

CONCLUSION: THE PERSECUTION OF
THE CHURCH AND ITS CAUSES

LET us now consider the motive for these persecutions, which cannot be separated from the no less terrible attacks made on the secular clergy and on devout lay folk or from the destruction of the churches and the refusal to open those which remain unharmed. There is, I think, no doubt whatever that, though such factors as anti-clericalism,[1] avarice, greed[2] and the pure love of destruction so characteristic of Anarchism[3] enter into any comprehensive discussion of this question, the underlying motive, responsible both for the features peculiar to this particular persecution and for its unexampled ferocity, is hatred of God.

The brief historical sketch of the development of the attacks on the Church given above has led us to this conclusion; and, quite independently of it, many who have no interest in Spanish politics have given it as their opinion that no other conclusion can be drawn from the facts. But some readers of this book will for political reasons—reasons which one can fully understand and respect—be convinced of the justice of the Popular Front's cause, and these are unwilling to associate the cause with an attitude which they would entirely deprecate. Some of them, no doubt, have so completely made up their minds that nothing would convince them; others may be prepared, however unwillingly, to admit the force of overwhelming argument. For the sake of these last we shall first consider the reasons adduced

---

[1] Cf. the details of P. Murall's narrative (p. 173, above).
[2] Cf. *Catalonia Infelix*, p. 261. [3] *Ibid.*

by those who have denied or doubted that there is an anti-God movement in Spain and then the reasons for acknowledging its existence.

The arguments of those unable to see the anti-God movement in Spain are not very convincing. Most persons, indeed, who ascribe the outrages to anti-clericalism simply make the assertion, without attempting to prove it: so eager are only too many to believe such a statement, especially if it is made by an Anglican bishop, a distinguished scientist, a popular novelist or some authority in any other sphere than the one he is writing about that proof is presumably held to be unnecessary. Where argument is used in support of the assertion it generally seems to take such a form as this:

> Past attacks on the Church have been due to anti-clericalism;
> Fresh attacks have now been made on the Church:
> Therefore these fresh attacks are due to anti-clericalism.

Not long ago eighteen signatories to a letter in *The Times*—mainly Bishops, clergymen and Free Church ministers—made the following astounding assertion:

> Reference to Spanish history completely dispels the idea that anti-clerical outbreaks in Spain must be prompted by Communism, for they were familiar long before the day of Karl Marx.[1]

Where these writers learned their Spanish history it is difficult to imagine. Setting charitably aside their probably unintentional use of the question-begging epithet "anti-clerical," we answer that reference to nineteenth-century

[1] *The Times*, November 29, 1937. The writers were answered by Captain Ramsay on December 4 and by Lord Clonmore on December 21, 1937.

history proves nothing about twentieth-century outrages one way or the other but that reference to twentieth-century history proves irrefutably that the outrages were inspired to a very large extent either by Russian Communism, Marxism or the Libertarian Communism more commonly called Anarchism. About this there can be no kind of doubt.

Occasionally, however, a real attempt has been made to discover the truth, which deserves serious consideration. Into this category comes a paragraph in the "report of a group of Anglican and Free Churchmen who visited Spain, January 29 to February 9, 1937." The visit, however good the intentions behind it may have been, was in some respects an unfortunate one. But if among those responsible for it there were critics of the Church, there were undoubtedly also men whose earnest desire was to learn the true causes of the persecution. That delegates were sent who lacked the necessary qualifications for discovering those causes is both obvious and lamentable, but none the less with the qualifications they had they did their best and made out a plausible case for their theory:

> *"Anti-God" Propaganda.* We found no evidence of an organized "Godless" propaganda such as has existed in Soviet Russia. We were unable on enquiry to hear of any caricatures of God, of Christ, or of the Virgin and Saints, such as have been features of "anti-God" propaganda in other countries. On the other hand, members of our party found copies of the Scriptures offered freely for sale on street book-stalls. The situation in regard to religion in Spain was summed up to us by a very acute English observer of dispassionate views, one who knows Spain well and is himself a practising Catholic, in the following terms: "There is a strong anti-clerical movement, but no anti-God movement in Spain."[1]

[1] *Report of a Group of Anglican and Free Churchmen, etc.*, §1.

To the last sentence I attach no importance whatsoever: another "very acute English observer" with exactly similar qualifications would have told them the contrary. To produce the opinions of anonymous informants is not to conduct a first-hand investigation. The other two statements deserve examination.

1. *They found no evidence of organized "Godless" propaganda?*[1] Then they could not have looked very far. They could not have read any large number of newspapers of the type of *Solidaridad Obrera*, nor Anarchist and Communist pamphlets which were common enough in Spain long before the War —I once saw some for sale, during the Republic, on the steps of a Cathedral.

They could not hear of caricatures of God? Where could they have searched for them? Here at home, receiving at that time perhaps an average of eight or ten left-wing newspapers a week, I was able within a few days of reading this singular statement to collect from a pile of these papers a dozen such caricatures. Among their authors was the respectable caricaturist, Bagaria, whose newspaper, before the War, was so moderate in its Republicanism that left-wing extremists used to say it had been bought by the Jesuits. Even the staid old *Vanguardia* of Barcelona demeaned itself by printing such caricatures.

No caricatures of Christ, of the Virgin and the Saints? Even supposing the writers failed to observe or understand the scribblings on walls some of which have been preserved by being photographed, could they possibly have failed to see such authenticated photographs as that of the statue of the Child Jesus decked in a red cap and brandishing a pistol, of that of the Virgin in militia dress—both these from Madrid churches—or of those of Christ and of His Mother, the eyes of which have been deliberately gouged out and

[1] Though they avow (§3) that "there had grown up in Spain a section which believed in violence and terrorism, and whose activities were specially directed against the Church *and the observance of religion.*" (Italics mine.)

other features disfigured with malicious care? Or what of the assault made on the statue of Christ on the Hill of the Angels? Or, again: "I had sworn to be revenged on You," said a Communist to Our Lord in the Tabernacle; and, aiming a pistol at Him, he fired on Him, saying: "Surrender to the Reds! Surrender to Marxism!"[1]

Did all this denote respect and reverence for Our Lord? Was this mere anti-clericalism?

Naturally the party could not hear of these things "on enquiry": those of whom they enquired, and whose guests they were, had every reason for withholding them. But they might have done a little more independent investigation.

2. The point about the Bibles being offered for sale is a much more subtle one. I do not doubt for a moment that this was a fact and that it might have been observed in many large towns under Popular Front rule.[2] The position of the Bible in Spain is one that has interested me for nearly a quarter of a century. When I first visited Madrid, well primed by militant Protestantism with the Black Legend, I was surprised to find that one could buy a Bible almost anywhere and that cheap editions of it were advertised freely in the Press and even on railway-stations and in street-cars. Having discovered that Catholic Spain was in no sense a Bible-less Spain, I began to investigate the position of the Bible from the other side and tried to find out what those who professed no religious beliefs thought of it. And from conversations, not only with anti-clericals but with free-thinkers and agnostics, I gradually deduced the fact that the Bible is regarded by such people with what might be called a strictly detached respect. They view it as they would a religious painting or a Gothic Cathedral— as something tainted with superstition, but undoubtedly worthy of respect, principally because it has some kind of

[1] *Joint Letter*, p. 21.
[2] Similar testimony has since been published in *The Tablet* (D. J. Collier: "A Catholic Doctor in Barcelona," October 15, 1938).

relation with what everybody in Spain reverences, even if he has not the slightest understanding of it: *cultura*.

Having discovered this long before the War began, I was not surprised to find, not only that, during the War, a party of foreigners had seen Bibles offered for sale in Spain, but (at a later date) that the Bible was actually being featured at the 1937 Barcelona Book Fair.[1] Here is the translation of a display advertisement inserted by the Sociedad Bíblica (British and Foreign Bible Society) in a number of Barcelona papers at that time, offering a Bible containing 1,248 pages and several coloured maps for 7 pesetas (equivalent, before the War, to about 3s. 6d.).

BIBLE
OLD AND NEW TESTAMENTS

This book is the foundation of our culture. ¶ It abounds in biographies of notable men and women. ¶ It tells us the bitter but wholesome truth. ¶ It comforts and guides us in daily life. ¶ It contains the wonderful life and redemptive death of Jesus. ¶ It leads our spirits to God.

The first two of these six recommendations, to which the Bible Society so prudently gives pride of place, are those chiefly to be noted. It was not so much because the Bible is the Word of God that a Government containing Anarchists and Communists allowed it to be advertised and sold

---

[1] The British and Foreign Bible Society reported the sale of 470 volumes (Bibles, New Testaments and separate books of the Bible) in the three days (June 3–5, 1937) of this Fair. Its total sales in Barcelona from July 1936 to February 1937 were 3,498 volumes. Total sales throughout Spain during 1937 were 36,202 volumes, comparing creditably with the 305,305 of 1935, and the 211,286 of 1936; and, during the first three months of 1938, 36 more copies of the complete Bible were sold than during the whole of 1937.

freely in June 1937 as because it abounds in biographies of notable men and women and is the foundation of our culture. And, happily, for that reason, it will continue to be advertised and sold, even if the Popular Front should win the War, until (in that event) the anti-God movement, at present vague in its nature and widely dispersed, is properly organized and put in the forefront of the programme of an Anarchist or a Communist *régime*. And even then it will be the last relic of Christianity to go, and it will go amid protests from members of the victorious party—from those of them, that is to say, who enjoy reading biographies and believe in culture.

In passing, it may be remarked here that it is extremely unwise to base hasty conclusions upon the attitude of any individual Spaniard to anything concerning religion. Before drawing inferences from isolated facts, one needs to know the people very well—and the better one knows them the more one hesitates to generalize. Two incidents, how-ever, will illustrate the tenacity of the religious instinct, which is often smouldering when it seems to be quite extinguished.

Cardinal Gomá, in one of his pastorals, tells how, some years ago, a motor-coach was overturned on its way back from a political meeting. In the coach was a party of twenty-four left-wing extremists, all of whom were killed. When the bodies were extricated, it was found that each of the men had around his neck a medal with its image of Christ or the Virgin worn by every Spanish Catholic.[1] The second incident is reproduced[2] from the Republican and anti-clerical *El Diluvio*, of Barcelona. At the beginning of May 1937 a correspondent of this paper at the front, himself an unbeliever, describes how he helped a dying man to recite the Lord's Prayer.

"What can I do for you?" he had asked him.

[1] Gomá, II, 45.   [2] Carreras, p. 229.

And the reply he received had been:

"Tell my mother I am thinking of her. I want to say the Lord's Prayer and I can't remember it. . . ."

The Spanish Bishops tell us that "the vast majority of our Communists have at the moment of death been reconciled to the God of their fathers."[1] No one who knows Spain, and realizes how deeply the Catholic faith is enrooted in her peoples, can be surprised at that, and one is glad to think that at the supreme moment instincts assert themselves which go deeper than intellectual beliefs.

But there are stranger facts than this to be explained by any who think the question now being discussed is a simple one. There are, for example, two incidents vouched for by Cardinal Gomá: in one parish a meeting to express adherence to the Third International began with a General Communion in church; in another, Labour Day was ushered in with a solemn Mass for all parishioners.[2] There is also the type of man who tells you that he disbelieves in God but believes implicitly in the Sacrament of the Altar or in the Virgin of the Pillar. There is the story of the man who emerged from an ugly-looking crowd which was threatening a Holy Week street procession in Seville. "I am a Communist and an atheist," he is alleged to have cried, brandishing a pistol, "but, by God, if one of you lays a finger on this statue of Our Lady I'll shoot him dead!" The Spaniard is not by nature a logical machine and it is quite in keeping with his nature that the anti-God movement in Spain should reveal these inconsistencies. Even the atheism of Spanish Anarchists may not be as deeply rooted as it seems. Bakunin himself, as a young man, was a mystically minded romantic, full of immortal longings—it was just that at the cross-roads of his life he took the wrong turning. Who can tell how many Spaniards just now professing a fanatical atheism are not also mystics at heart?

[1] *Joint Letter*, p. 22.   [2] Gomá, II, 118.

They have been induced, it is true, by skilful propaganda to make a transfer of allegiance; but when happier times come to their country they will perhaps be won back to a faith which has been clouded over in their souls but never destroyed.

We come now to the proofs of the anti-God movement's existence. At present, it must be understood, the movement is ill-defined, widely and unequally spread over the territory held by the Popular Front, and limited in its opportunities of self-expression by the preferential claim on extremist activity of the War and the Proletarian Revolution. The evidence for its existence can best be classified under three headings.

I. *Historical reasons.*—These alone seem quite conclusive. The narrative detailed above, covering some two hundred years, shows how the first attacks made upon the Church in the period which it describes were inspired by Bourbon regalism, and how as a secondary motive came the State's desire to possess the wealth of the Church, at that time very considerable. Gradually this latter motive became dominant, and the Church's uncompromising and perhaps too insensitive opposition to liberalism and those who professed it was the chief factor in the development of a third motive —anti-clericalism—which was responsible for most of the persecution of the Church during the first half of the nineteenth century. But, although among the leaders of this persecution there were prominent free-thinkers and atheists, it was not until the latter part of the century that the anti-God movement began, first in the form of Anarchism and later in that of Communism, and not until well into the twentieth century that this movement assumed really large proportions. As early as 1931, the Anarcho-Syndicalist Unions claimed a membership of over one million—one-fifteenth, let us say, of the adult population of the country. By no means all these members, of course, would subscribe to the anti-God principles of the Iberian Anarchist Federation, but the Federation infused into Syndicalism a very strong leaven and this was reinforced by the leaven of Russian Communism, the attitude of which to the Christian religion under any of its forms it is unnecessary to describe.

During the last two decades I have myself seen something of the gradual transformation of the anti-clerical movement into the anti-God movement. There are two brands of anti-clericalism. The first is quite mild and good-natured, in evidence chiefly among men of the middle classes; though it has an influence on attendance at Divine worship, it does not greatly affect religious belief, and it is seldom combative, still less destructive. In England it is represented by the type of man who doesn't hold with parsons and communes with God on Sundays in bed or on the golf-links while his family goes to church. The other kind is very different. It is fostered, by agitators, among the poor, and feeds on grievances of which in all conscience the poor have enough, and which agitators have persuaded them are in some way or other the fault of the clergy. This anti-clericalism obviously provides an excellent foundation for Anarchist and Communist doctrines and it is because there were so many anti-clericals of this type that the anti-God movement has made, especially since 1931, such rapid progress.

We come, then, to this conclusion. The fuel heaped upon the fires which have burned so fiercely may have consisted in large measure of anti-clericalism. But fuel alone does not make a fire—it needs a match to ignite it. And the match which has ignited the fuel gathered with ever-increasing assiduity during the last seven years is nothing less than hatred of God.

II. *Characteristics of the persecution.*—Let us now try to assess the nature of the persecutions of 1936–7 with all possible objectivity. Do they look like persecutions inspired by hatred of the clergy among people who are Christians at have been new forms of torture which modern invention and machinery have made possible.

"Hatred of Jesus Christ and the Blessed Virgin has reached the state of paroxysm; and from the hundreds of crucifixes which have been slashed with knives, from the images of the Virgin bestially profaned, from the Bilbao lampoons sacrilegiously blaspheming the Mother of God, from the vile literature of the Red trenches, mocking the Divine mysteries, from the repeated profanation of the Sacred Host, we can deduce what hell-like hatred is incarnated in our unhappy Communists.

"We do not believe," they write further, "that the entire history of Christianity can show a period of only a few weeks in which has occurred such an explosion of hatred, in all forms of thought, will, and passion, against Jesus Christ and His sacred religion. So terrible were the sacrilegious ravages suffered by the Church in Spain that the delegate sent by the Spanish Reds to the Congress of the Godless in Moscow was able to say: 'Spain has far surpassed the work of the Soviets, for the Church in Spain has been completely annihilated.' "[1]

Dislike of the clerical system will no doubt inspire a resolute determination to oppose it in every possible way; it may even cause, and has in the past caused, explosions of feeling, and hot-blooded crimes, of which the authors might afterwards be ashamed. But it could hardly inspire a calculated large-scale policy of incendiarism and murder, extending over many weeks, and sparing neither aged nor infirm, women nor children. Men do not rape and murder frightened nuns in lay clothing who have taken refuge in private houses because of their dislike of the clerical system. Only some passion which takes possession of them and makes

---

[1] *Op. cit.*, p. 20. Cf. Carreras, pp. 64, 153. "I spent eighteen months in Russia," one of the men smashing images in Vich Cathedral was heard to say, "and they taught us there how to do things. We learned to hate Christ and to make war on Him to the death. We won't leave a single cross standing."

more than 1,190 communicants.[1] The Anarchists, who appear chiefly to be responsible for the continued closing of the churches, would hardly be aware of their existence: certainly such small bodies would not be worth seeking out and persecuting in war-time, especially as they met in inconspicuous chapels or even in private houses. But there is a counter-objection to be made. If the Anarchists have intentionally excepted the Protestants from their persecution of religion, why have they never said so? In no book or article written by an Anarchist, a Syndicalist or a Communist author have I ever found so much as a reference to Protestant Evangelicals. What the Anarcho-Communists say (quoting Marx) is that *religion*—not Catholicism—is the opium of the people.[2] Precisely; and if the Popular Front should win the War, and the Anarchists or the Communists sweep away the Republican parties, as they have expressed their intention of doing when the Revolution of the People is triumphant, we shall see if Protestants are excepted from the universal ban which, as Anarchists have told us, they propose to place upon the practice of religion. What sort of treatment, we may enquire, have Protestant Evangelicals received in Soviet Russia?

Why, again, if the Anarchists are opposed not to religion but only to clerical dominance, did they not agree to a general opening of the churches? That the Republican parties would have been only too glad to open them, at an early stage in the War, goes without saying: whether or no they have themselves any use for religion, they are quite naturally most eager to do anything which will conciliate opinion[3] and remove the just and natural criticism that they

---

[1] Cf. also p. 4, above.

[2] "It is . . . useless to deny that both Anarchism and Marxian Socialism are hostile to all religion," admits one of the franker supporters of the Popular Front (George Orwell, in *New English Weekly*, November 24, 1938).

[3] Cf. the statement made by members of the Popular Front Government "with one voice" in January 1937 (*Report of a Group of Anglican and Free Churchmen, etc.*, § 5). The sixth of the thirteen points enunciated on May 1, 1938,

are contravening the terms of their own Constitution.[1] It can only be fear of creating discord between their allies that restrains them.

Continually they make attempts to restore some degree of liberty of worship and then retreat from them. More than a year after the outbreak of war, for example, on August 15, 1937, the Feast of the Assumption, which fell on a Sunday, a Mass was celebrated at Valencia, on the premises of the delegation of the Basque Government, and another at Madrid, in an "official building transformed into a chapel for the occasion."[2] The comments of the extremist Press during the week were not encouraging. *Mundo Obrero*, a Communist paper, reported that the Government considered any declaration "inopportune" and hinted that no more would be heard of it.[3] The Anarcho-Syndicalist organ, *C.N.T.*, asked for "a little respect for the victims who fell before the weapons brandished by priests and monks, by Jesuits and Catholic Fascists who fired from convents and churches."[4] In spite of these and many other criticisms, it was announced on August 21 that "Roman Catholic churches will reopen for public services throughout Republican Spain on Sunday," and at the same time, somewhat contradictorily but on the authority of the Minister of

by Dr. Negrín, Prime Minister of the Republican Government, as the Government's official policy, guarantees "to all citizens . . . liberty of conscience and the free exercise of religious belief and practice." Again, on the second anniversary of the outbreak of War, Dr. Negrín said: "No obstacles shall be encountered in Republican Spain by men of any faith, whether Catholic or Protestant, to their professing their religious beliefs" (*The Times*, July 19, 1938). Many similar statements could be quoted, but it is one thing to promise, and another, when one is not one's own master, to perform.

[1] Article 27 of this (1931) Constitution guarantees to the individual freedom of conscience and permits him to profess and practise any form of religion provided it does not transgress public morals. The Anarcho-Syndicalists and Communists, of course, would not consider themselves bound by this "paper Constitution" (cf. *Catalonia Infelix*, p. 291), but it is hard to see how moderate Republican supporters of the Popular Front, who still profess allegiance to the Constitution, can justify the attitude taken by their successive Governments to public worship.

[2] The phrase is taken from the Press Association report which appeared in the British Press of August 16, 1937.

[3] *Mundo Obrero*, August 21, 1937.   [4] *C.N.T.*, August 18, 1937.

Justice, that "the churches would be reopened within six weeks."[1]

This sounded altogether too much like *mañana* to be credible. And one's misgivings were justified. The churches were not reopened, and this despite pressure from the Popular Front's Basque supporters, for whom even those who regret their political affiliation must feel sympathy. When, on October 30, 1937, the Government moved from Valencia to Barcelona, the Basque refugees, good Catholics who had lost all by supporting the Popular Front, begged the Minister of Justice, himself a Basque, to open *one* church for them in the Catalan capital, so that they might once more have the consolations of religion. They pointed out "that 20,000 Basques had died in the course of the War for the cause of Euzkadi and its age-long liberties, dominant among which are religious liberty and freedom of conscience"; that thousands more were still fighting for the Republic in Aragon; and that their loyalty could not therefore be suspect. The opportunities provided for Divine worship in private, they said, were quite insufficient. Even on the battlefield, they had been enabled to perform their religious duties: should they not have at least equal facilities so far behind the lines? Finally, they pointed out—one hardly knows whether there is more of pathos or of irony in this contention—that their petition in no way conflicted with the Constitution, which guaranteed freedom of worship to all, as did "the Liberal policy followed by the Government." The Minister promised to submit the question to the Cabinet. But nothing happened.[2]

Still the Basques persisted and still the Government said, "Not yet, but quite soon." In March 1938 *The Times* Correspondent reported from Barcelona that "Sunday worship," provided it took place "in private, behind closed

[1] *Daily Telegraph*, August 21, 1937.
[2] *La Vanguardia*, November 20, 1937; *The Times*, November 23, 1937.

doors," was "no longer punishable."[1] The most the Basques could achieve, however, was permission for several Masses to be said daily in the chapel of their own Government building,[2] and later, on Sundays, in a small chapel in the Calle de Pino. Other services had for some time been held in chapels and private houses (all "behind closed doors"), though once again the Minister of Justice promised that *muy pronto* ("very soon") these chapels "should be converted into public places of worship."[3] Nine months have passed since then and still this has not been done—after two and a half years of the War.[4]

The next move in the direction of tolerance for religious belief and practice was made in June 1938, when an official order authorized the granting, on active service, of "all possible facilities to those who wish to receive spiritual aid from the ministers of the religion which they profess, who may . . . within the limits imposed by active service, freely exercise the practices of their respective cults."[5] This is excellent as far as it goes, but of course leaves the main question completely untouched.

The same may be said of an incident which occurred on October 17, 1938, and was given by the propagandist sheets a significant degree of publicity. On this date, it appears, a Basque Captain who had been killed at the front was given a Catholic funeral. A robed priest is said to have walked in the procession, followed by two Cabinet Ministers and a large concourse of people. That such an occurrence, so

---

[1] *The Times*, March 2, 1938.   [2] *Ibid.*

[3] "Conversación con el Ministro Sr. Irujo," reported in the propagandist sheet entitled *Servicio Español de Información*, Barcelona, March 14, 1938.

[4] Much the same story can be told of Madrid. Again and again it has been said that churches will be opened *muy pronto*. During the second half of November 1938, the propagandist sheets came out with the information that "a church will soon be opened in Madrid." The statement is attributed to Father Leocadio Lobo, who, before making it, "had just baptized a child," giving it the (very appropriate) name of María del Milagro. "I believe," continues the statement, "that, within a month, I shall be able to celebrate the Divine Service openly in the church called San Antonio de los Alemanes. This will be the first church fully reopened in Madrid."

[5] *La Publicitat*, Barcelona, June 28, 1938.

ordinary in normal times, as the burial of an individual according to the rites of his Faith should have excited this amount of comment illustrates the intensity with which religion has been persecuted. Every attempt, indeed, made to represent the situation in the best possible light does this, and the most it proves is that conditions are very slowly, almost imperceptibly, improving.[1]

What might be a greater advance was announced by propagandist sheets and the left-wing Press on December 10, 1938, in the shape of a decree "formally reaffirming the principle of religious freedom in Republican Spain" and appointing a "Commissary-General of Worship" who will have "the necessary powers for the re-establishment of religious worship."[2] It is too early to say how far, if at all, this "reaffirmation" of what, had the Republican Constitution been enforced, would have needed no reaffirmation, is likely to prove effective. After two and a half years' prohibition of public worship, Spanish Christians may perhaps be forgiven if they attach no great importance to the words *muy pronto* while the churches still remain closed.

The reasons given by supporters of the Popular Front for this prohibition—fear of Fascist plots and the like—are altogether too futile to be taken seriously. From the very beginning of the Proletarian Revolution it would have been

[1] Dr. D. J. Collier (*The Tablet*, October 15, 1938: see also correspondence in following issues) writes a description of a story in Barcelona during the preceding summer which is intended to convey the impression that the improvement, in that city, is much greater than is generally believed. She was "assured that no one need have any difficulty about attending Mass on Sundays or week-days; much is expected in the next few months"; and " 'If you are here in two months' time [*muy pronto*!] you will probably find things different,' a leader of the Federacio de Joves Cristianos [*sic*] told me." But Dr. Collier has to confirm the fact that the churches were not opened for public worship: she herself attended Mass in "a private house," "a hall" and "the Basque chapel." Priests, she tells us, are dressed as laymen (Why?), and nuns in secular attire, questioned about their religious dress, replied "that there was no objection to this, but as the habits were rather hot, they were waiting for the cold weather before resuming them." This last answer is worth preserving.

[2] *Manchester Guardian*, December 10, 1938. Cf. Appendix IV.

simple for the Government, instead of allowing churches to be used as garages, refuse-dumps and markets, to open for worship the principal church or churches in each town and to arrange that Masses should be said there at a fixed hour daily. The officiating priests might have been selected with ease from the vast number which (so we are informed) supports the Popular Front.[1] Armed police stationed at intervals inside the building and posted in force outside would be able to prevent both Fascist conspiracies and any kind of disturbance, or even to enforce complete silence. The true reasons for the closing of the churches must be sought elsewhere and unfortunately they lie only too near at hand.

III. *Testimony of Anarchists.*—If the Popular Front should win the War, and either Anarchism or Communism should gain the ascendancy over moderate Republicanism, we may be sure that the anti-God movement, at present subordinated to the anti-Franco movement, will fill the centre of the victors' activities. There will then be ample testimony to the motives behind the persecution. At present such testimony appears but rarely, and then almost exclusively in the Anarchists' own organs, such as *Solidaridad Obrera*, so that it is seen but little by the general public.

Three examples of this frank admission that it is religion and not merely clericalism, or even Catholicism, which is being attacked, I have quoted in a recent book, *Catalonia Infelix*. They may be briefly referred to here.

The first is an article from the newspaper just named,[2] which was published, under the apt title, "The Mask and the Face," shortly after Sr. Álvarez del Vayo had assured the League of Nations that if the Popular Front won the

[1] "There are in Barcelona at this moment," writes Dr. Hewlett Johnson (*Manchester Guardian*, June 16, 1938), "at least 2,000 Catholic priests, and no hindrance is placed by the Government on the public [*sic*] performance of their priestly functions." Dr. Collier, in October (*art. cit.*), raises this number to 3,000 and propagandist sheets give still higher figures.
[2] *Solidaridad Obrera*, January 28, 1937.

War Spain would again enjoy the freedom of worship. "This kind of promise or engagement of Álvarez del Vayo's to re-establish Catholic worship," says the writer, "may have sounded well in the League of Nations. But here, in Spain, it has only made us smile."

No movement directed against the Church can be too violent. Religion in a nation is an incurable disease. Lenin [sic] said that religion was opium. He should have gone farther. Opium enervates and lulls to sleep. Little by little it saps man's organic energies. But it is only physical. Religion enters the very marrow of the spirit, the life of what "they" call the soul; it makes its home there like a microbe and slowly destroys the personality. At the end of the life of one of these creatures captured by the Church, nothing remains to him of his own being.

We hardly know how far it is possible to talk of "freedom of worship"—we who know the harm done by religion. "Freedom to do harm" is much too liberal a principle. If we deny people freedom to become drunk, to prostitute themselves, to commit suicide, are we to give them freedom to become fanatics? . . . The people did well to begin by committing the churches to the flames; and the flames, without a doubt, will devour all the churches except by some miracle. . . .

The second quotation is from *Umbral*—no working-class periodical but a high-grade illustrated newspaper published in Valencia. The very title of the article is eloquent as to its inspiration. "This can never return," it is called—and below the words appears a photograph of a giant statue of the Christ with outstretched arms. It is the Christ, worshipped in the churches they have destroyed, whom these Anarchists are attacking. "Let us outlaw the Church, as has been done in Mexico," is the writer's conclusion. "Let us seize this unique moment which the actions of the masses have offered us so that the churches which they have burned may never be rebuilt."[1]

Thirdly come some quotations from a book published by an Anarchist leader, Juan Peiró—a book which takes us right into the heart of Anarchism with its glorification of direct action, revolution, bloodshed and destruction for destruction's sake. The revolutionary must go forward relentlessly: "if either persons or things stand in his way they must be ruthlessly sacrificed or razed to the very ground." "To kill those whom it is necessary to kill is an imperative revolutionary command."

> To kill as one would wish to kill would mean something like the assassinations which once bathed the streets of Barcelona with blood, when men were killed . . . for their ideas. . . . To kill God himself, if he existed . . . would be perfectly human and natural.[2]

Against the clerical system or against God?

Surely the title of the first article quoted answers the question. The anti-clerical mask, which so effectively deceived the "group of Anglican and Free Churchmen" and has been penetrated by few of the Popular Front's honest supporters, hides the anti-God face, from which, if all goes as the Anarchists hope, it will one day be flung off completely. That that day may never come, and that the whole of Spain may soon once more have freedom of worship, must be the wish of all—whether Catholic or Protestant—who love the Lord Jesus in sincerity, as well as of all who, though professing no religion themselves, hold that nothing is more deserving of respect than the religious beliefs of others.

[1] *Umbral*, July 31, 1937.   [2] Cf. *Catalonia Infelix*, p. 292.

APPENDIX I

THE WEALTH OF THE CHURCH IN SPAIN: AN ENQUIRY

Fantastic and patently ridiculous as are many of the statements that have been made about the Church's alleged wealth, I have thought it of interest to attempt to track some of them to their Spanish sources. In all I have investigated seven cases, without having obtained satisfactory evidence from a single one of them.

Case I.

In November 1937 a Scottish newspaper reported a speaker—a man who has studied Spain for many years and whose name, among Hispanists, commands general respect—as having

> described the Church in Spain as no longer a religious body, but rather a commercial, industrial and political entity. It might be news to them that the Church owned the biggest bank in Madrid, besides thirty-five agricultural banks, big businesses, cinemas, newspapers, a wireless station, and so on.

It was certainly news to me, except for the reference to what are called "agricultural banks," which indicates a benevolent scheme no more "commercial" than many which in Protestant countries command universal approval. So I wrote to ask the speaker if he would supply me with documentary proof that the Church in Spain owned:

(1) the biggest bank in Madrid,
(2) big businesses,
(3) cinemas,
(4) newspapers,
(5) a wireless station,

and give me the names of each. He answered that the words "biggest bank" should read "—— Bank, Capital, £5,000,000." I replied that that was quite big enough. At the end of two months, my correspondent said that he had been unable to trace the source of his statement about the Bank but had found that of the other statement—the report of a lecture, given in London in May 1936, which said that the Jesuits, according to "reliable statistics," now [*sic*][1] controlled the following:

> Eight banks.
> About 35 business enterprises of big scale.
> One powerful wireless station.
> A news agency.
> More than 60 newspapers in Madrid and the provinces.
> A good many theatres and cinemas.

On January 15, 1938, I wrote to the lecturer asking for his authority. He replied on February 3 that he could not find it, but would try again. I have heard nothing more from him about it since.

Case II.

The author of a pamphlet on the Civil War stated that "the Catholic Church of Spain . . . operated hotels and factories, owned department stores, numerous electric power plants, newspapers, etc."

On January 27, 1938, I wrote to him asking for "an authoritative, preferably a Spanish, source" for these statements, and also "the names of the hotels, factories, stores, etc., referred to."

To this letter I have received no reply.

Case III.

In *The Listener* for January 19, 1938, a correspondent referred to the Church, "which was the largest landowner in Spain, which owned or controlled such things as the tramway system of Madrid and the Bank of the Holy Ghost (one of the biggest in Spain)."

On January 26, another correspondent pointed out that the Banco Espirito Santo was a Portuguese, not a Spanish, concern, apparently without ecclesiastical connections, and asked the original correspondent to "furnish any information in support of his statements." No reply appeared.

I had also written asking him for proof that "the Catholic

[1] The Society of Jesus had, as we have seen, been dissolved in Spain in February 1932.

Church (*a*) was the largest landowner in Spain, (*b*) controlled the tramway system of Madrid." No reply was received.

Case IV.

On February 12, 1938, a propagandist sheet published a long series of statements about the Church in Spain, some of which are quoted in the text above. Certain of the statements were clearly erroneous: *e.g.*, that "the Spanish clergy, a veritable army of occupation, numbered 106,734 persons! (25,474 priests and 81,260 monks and nuns)":[1] for the correct figures see p. 206, below. The statements were attributed to "a Catholic."

I asked the Editor for the source of his information and for documentary proofs. He replied that to provide these last was impossible, but sent the names of four Spanish books which dealt with the facts. Two of these books I have been unable to obtain; the other two give no evidence in support of the statements made. The Editor added that the "Catholic" did not "wish his name to be disclosed."

Case V.

On February 17, 1938, I wrote to an author who had stated (*a*) that there were 106,734 clergy and religious in Spain; (*b*) that the "Jesuit order . . . owned the Banco —— in Madrid" and "controlled four smaller provincial banks with a total capital of 85,000,000 pesetas." I asked for the sources of these statements.

In reply, I was referred for (*b*) to a propagandist sheet of 1931. I wrote to the author of this for his sources but received no reply, For (*a*) I was told that the source was an American magazine, but my informant "could not now confirm which issue."

Case VI.

On February 17, 1938, I asked for sources from an author who had written that (*a*) the Church "controlled banks and industrial

---

[1] It is a common practice of those who decry the Orders in Spain to exaggerate the numbers of religious. The Duchess of Atholl (*Searchlight on Spain*, 3rd ed., p. 26) also makes them, in my opinion, too large by some 60,000. The numbers as given by a Republican Minister will be found in Appendix II. It will be seen that the figures given here and under Case V are true of the eighteenth, and not of the twentieth, century. Even Mr. Brinton, who gives the relatively modest estimate of "about 85,000' '(*Christianity and Spain*, p. 18), nearly doubles the figures of this Minister.

concerns, owned urban house property"; (*b*) "until 1936 the tramway system in Madrid belonged to the Church"; (*c*) the Church had "considerable sums invested in banking, industry and even in large scale commercial undertakings and shipping."

The reply was that these statements were based, not on published sources, but on information given by the Press Department of the Ministerio del Estado in Madrid, in private conversations, etc.

Case VII.

An author who had written: "It was pointed out in the Cortes in 1931 that the Jesuits owned one-third of the total wealth of Spain," was asked when this was pointed out, by whom and on what authority. The author could not answer these questions but gave as authority for the statement (*a*) "a man whom I met in Bilbao in 1932. I do not recall his name; I had reason to think that he could be relied upon for his facts and I made a note of what he said"; (*b*) a pamphlet "by some pro-Government writer."

APPENDIX II

TWO CENTURIES OF SPANISH CHURCH HISTORY: A SUMMARY (1737-1937)

1737. First attempt made to establish a Concordat between Church and State.

1753. Effective Concordat drawn up.

1767. Expulsion of Jesuits from Spain (Suppression of the Society: 1773-1814).

1798. First expropriation law enacted under Charles IV, compensation being given.

1805. The Pope allows Charles IV to sell further Church property, compensation being given.

1808. Napoleon Bonaparte decrees reduction of religious houses by two-thirds.

1809. Joseph Bonaparte suppresses all religious houses and seizes their property. Decrees resisted—Bishop of Coria and others murdered—Solsona Cathedral burned down.

1812. Cortes of Cádiz suppress the smaller religious houses, etc. Protesting Bishops exiled or suspended. Papal Nuncio expelled.

1814. Ferdinand VII annuls the above-named measures.

1815. Return of Jesuits.

1820-3. Liberal triennium inaugurated by revolt of Riego. Suppression of numerous Orders and all small or isolated religious houses. Suspension of certain benefices and reduction of the number of parish priests. Ordinations forbidden. Secularization of Church property. Expulsion of Jesuits. Bishops ordered to proclaim 1812 Constitution. Assassinations and violence. Murder of Bishop of Vich.

1823. Annulment of above-named measures. Return of Jesuits.

1834 (July 17). Anti-clerical riot in Madrid. Murder of priests, religious and laymen.

1835 (April–July). Anti-clerical riots in Saragossa, Murcia, Barcelona, Reus, Tarragona, Valencia, Majorca, Málaga and Salamanca.

(July 4). Dissolution of Society of Jesus in Spain.

(July 25). Suppression of 900 religious houses.

(October 11). Mendizábal's emergency decree suppressing (with a few exceptions) all religious houses and seizing their property.

1836 (February 19, March 5, 9). Further suppressions of religious houses. Seizure and sale of their property.

1837 (April 27). Promulgation of 1837 Constitution, imposing upon the State the responsibility for Divine worship. Suppression of all religious houses except those of Escolapian and Hospitaller Orders. Confiscation of property both of regulars and of seculars. Abolition of tithes and first-fruits (July 29). Persecution and expulsion of Bishops. Vacant sees left unfilled.

1840. After a brief interlude of moderate government, the sale of the property of the secular clergy is resumed. The Papal Vicegerent protests and is expelled from the country.

1843. Moderate decade begins. Incumbents reinstated. New Bishops consecrated. Ordinations resumed. New measure voted for maintenance of Divine worship.

1844. Sale of property of secular clergy suspended. Unsold residue returned to its owners.

1845. Concordat with Rome drafted but proves unacceptable to the Government.

1851 (October 17). Concordat promulgated.

1854–5. "Progressive" ("luckless") biennium.

1855 (May 1). Disentailment Law passed. Smaller convents suppressed and admission of novices to convents forbidden.

1856. Scope of expropriation extended.

1856 (October). The above laws of 1855–6 repealed.

1860. Convenio (supplementary to 1851 Concordat) passed between the Holy See and the Spanish Government.

1868. Revolution: Isabel II dethroned. Revolutionary Junta

suppresses all religious communities established since 1837, dissolves the Society of Jesus and the Order of St. Vincent of Paul in Spain, and reduces convents by one-half, giving no compensation. Riots and church-burnings in Madrid, Barcelona, Reus, Huesca, Valladolid, Salamanca, Palencia, Seville, etc.

1869. Constitution of 1869 promulgated.

1873–5. First Republic. Riots and church-burnings at Málaga, Cádiz, Palencia, Barcelona, etc.

1875. Accession of Alfonso XII.

1876. Constitution of 1876 promulgated. Concordat of 1851 again in force.

1887. Law of Associations passed.

1901 (September 19). Alfonso González requires religious Orders to register under the Law of Associations.

1902. Difficulties arising from this resolved by a *modus vivendi.*

1904. New Convenio drafted and passes Senate but fails to pass Congress.

1906. New Law of Associations drafted but fails to pass the Cortes.

1909. "Tragic Week" in Barcelona. Sixty-three churches and religious houses burned down.

1910. "Padlock Law" passed.

1911. New Law of Associations drafted but fails to pass the Cortes.

1931–6. Second Republic (See pp. 126–62).

1936–37. Persecution of the Church following outbreak of the Civil War and the Proletarian Revolution (See pp. 163–98).

APPENDIX III

ESTIMATED NUMBERS OF RELIGIOUS IN SPAIN

(i) From 1700 to 1835

Date	Men	Women	Total	Authority
1700	90,000	38,700	128,700	Morote: *Los Frailes*, etc., p. 42.
1753	70,000	30,000	100,000	Morote, *loc. cit.*
1768	55,435	27,665	83,100	Morote, *loc. cit.*
1787	52,300	25,365	77,665	La Fuente, VI, 462[1] Morote, *loc. cit.*
1796	53,098	24,007	77,105	Morote, *loc. cit.*
c.1801	59,768	33,630	93,398	Zabala, I, 198.
1803	61,327	31,400	92,727	Morote, p. 197, and Antequera: *Desamortización*, p. 455.
1809	49,238	22,347	71,585	Laborde, V, 15.
1826	37,363	23,552	60,915	Morote, *loc. cit.*
1830	?	?	61,727	La Fuente, VI, 481.
1833	?	?	55,279	Zabala, I, 199.
1835	31,000	22,000	53,000	Morote, *loc. cit.*[2]

(ii) From 1900 to 1931

Date	Men	Women	Total	Authority
1902	10,745	40,188	50,933	Fernández Almagro, p. 22.
1904	10,630	40,030	50,660	Morote, *loc. cit.*
1924	c.12,000	42,000	54,000	*Encyclopaedia Britannica.*
1928	10,270	38,961	49,231	Araujo & Grubb, pp. 44–5.
1931	8,396	36,569	44,965	Fernando de los Ríos, in Spanish Cortes, October 8, 1931.

[1] But Morote (p. 197) gives the numbers for 1788 from another source as 67,777 men and 32,640 women. Both these and his figures for 1787 can hardly be correct. Cf. also, on the discrepancies for this year, Parker, *The Catholic Church in Spain*, p. 16, n.

[2] For the same year, Brandt (p. 31: source of information apparently German) gives *c.* 30,000 men and *c.* 37,000 women.

APPENDIX IV

TEXT OF THE DECREE ISSUED BY THE POPULAR FRONT GOVERNMENT CREATING A COMMISSARIAT-GENERAL OF WORSHIP, DECEMBER 8, 1938

The Spanish Constitution, respecting as it does religious beliefs and sentiments to an extent which may be equalled, but is not surpassed, by the public law of any civilized country, solemnly establishes freedom of conscience and the right freely to profess and practise any form of religion.

These principles were developed in the law of June 2, 1933,[1] with the same breadth of spirit as that of the Constitution; and in the present circumstances, when the Spanish nation is energetically defending itself against attacks from without, the Government of the Republic reaffirms, as one of its war-aims, freedom of conscience and the free exercise of religious beliefs and practices.

It has certainly not been the spirit of freedom animating the Republic that has been responsible for the *de facto* situation which has brought about an abnormal state of affairs with reference to the practice of worship. The complete neglect, on the part of the leaders of the Church's hierarchy, of the social duties incumbent on members of every community—duties the observance of which is imposed by religious convictions themselves when these are firmly held—has led to public-spirited defensive reactions, which have operated in a sense contrary to this freedom. Furthermore, the exigencies of the war which the Spanish people are waging in defence of their independence have necessitated the occupation of buildings intended for worship and led to inevitable abnormalities in its practice.

The Government of the Republic has always endeavoured to inculcate the most delicate respect for religious convictions.

---

[1] This is the notorious "Law of Religious Congregations and Confessions," described on pp. 147–50, above, and in *The Spanish Tragedy*, pp. 123–4, 136–7.

Within the very Army which is serving the cause of national freedom, care has been taken to ensure the fulfilment of religious duties and the dispositions which have been issued with this end in view are of quite recent date.

In addition to doing this, the Government, being the organ of a country which is so dramatically and generously giving proof of its vocation for civilization and justice, is desirous of paving the way to normal conditions as to the practice of worship, according to the spirit of our Constitution.

In virtue of these considerations, by agreement with the Council of Ministers and on the proposal of its President, I issue the following decree:

ARTICLE I.—Within the Presidency of the Council of Ministers is hereby constituted a Commissariat-General of Worship (*Cultos*), which will deal with information, proposals and transactions on matters connected with the exercise of worship and the practice of religious activities in Spain.

ARTICLE II.—At the head of the Commissariat there shall be a Commissary-General, appointed by decree, on the nomination of the Presidency of the Council of Ministers; and to work with him there shall be a consultative committee composed of persons designated by the same Ministerial Department.

ARTICLE III.—The remaining Ministerial Departments, and especially those of Justice and Home Affairs, shall provide the data and information required by the Commissary-General of Worship.

ARTICLE IV.—Through the Ministry of Finance and Economy shall be provided the credits necessary for the requirements of the Commissariat of Worship.

ARTICLE V.—The Presidency of the Council of Ministers shall issue the dispositions necessary for the fulfilment of this decree.

Given at Barcelona, on the eighth day of December, 1938. MANUEL AZAÑA.—The President of the Council of Ministers: JUAN NEGRÍN LÓPEZ.

BIBLIOGRAPHY

ALTAMIRA Y CREVEA, RAFAEL: *Historia de España y de la civilización española* (3rd edition), Barcelona, 1913–14, 4 vols. [English edition, entitled: *A History of Spanish Civilization*, London, 1930].

ANON.: *La Persécution religieuse en Espagne*. Paris, 1937. [For authorship, see p. 170, above.]

ANON. (Burgos Correspondent of *The Tablet*): "The Church in Spain," in *The Tablet* (under different titles), November 12, 19, 26, December 3, 10, 1938.).

ANTEQUERA, J. M. DE: *La Desamortización Eclesiástica considerada en sus diferentes aspectos y relaciones*. Madrid, 1885. [Solid and substantial. The standard work on the subject from the Church standpoint.]

ANTEQUERA, J. M. DE: *La Doctrina Católica y la Escuela liberal*. Madrid, 1874. [A pamphlet.]

ANTEQUERA, J. M. DE: *Las Órdenes religiosas*. Madrid, 1880. [A pamphlet.]

ARAUJO GARCÍA, C. AND GRUBB, KENNETH G.: *Religion in the Republic of Spain*. London, 1933. [A Protestant Evangelical survey.]

BALMES, J. L.: *Escritos políticos (passim)*. Madrid, 1847–8, 2 vols.

BAYLE, P. CONSTANTINO, S.J.: *¿Qué pasa en España?* Salamanca, 1937. [A pamphlet.]

BOTELLA Y SERRA, CRISTÓBAL: *El Socialismo y los anarquistas*. Madrid, 1895.

BRANDT, JOSEPH A.: *Toward the New Spain*, Chicago, 1933.

BRINTON, HENRY: *Christianity and Spain*, London, 1938. [A pamphlet, which reprints as an Appendix the "Report of a Group of Anglican and Free Churchmen, etc.," referred to below.]

CARRERAS, P. LUIS: *Grandeza Cristiana de España: Notas sobre la persecución religiosa*. Toulouse, 1938.

CLARKE, H. BUTLER: *Modern Spain, 1815–1898*. Cambridge, 1906.

ELLIS, HAVELOCK: *The Soul of Spain*. London, 1908.

FERNÁNDEZ ALMAGRO, M.: *Historia del reinado de Alfonso XIII*. Barcelona, 1933.

GAMS, P. B., O.S.B.: *Die Kirchengeschichte von Spanien*. Regensburg, 1862–79, 3 vols.

GIL MAESTRE, M.: *El Anarquismo en España*. Madrid, 1897.

GOMÁ TOMÁS [Cardinal] I.: *Antilaicismo*. Barcelona, 1935, 2 vols. [Contains several important pastorals written during the Second Republic.]

GÜENECHEA, P. JOSÉ N., S.J.: *Pobreza del Culto y Clero en España*. Bilbao, 1916.

GUIXÉ, JUAN: *¿Qué ha hecho la República?, 1931–1933*. Madrid, 1933.

IZAGA, LUIS: *La Iglesia y el Estado*. Madrid, *Razón y Fe*, n.d.

Joint Letter of the Spanish Bishops to the Bishops of the whole world concerning the War in Spain. London, Catholic Truth Society, n.d. (Revised Edition, 1937.)

LABORDE, A. L. J. DE: *A View of Spain*. London, 1809, 5 vols. [Translated from the French. Vol. V has much information about the Church.]

LA FUENTE, V. DE: *Historia eclesiástica de España*. Barcelona, 1855 (later edition, 1873–5), 6 vols.

LANGDON-DAVIES, JOHN: *The Spanish Church and Politics*. London, 1937. [A pamphlet.]

LOEWENSTEIN, PRINCE HUBERTUS FRIEDRICH OF: *A Catholic in Republican Spain*. London, 1937. [A pamphlet.]

MADARIAGA, SALVADOR DE: *Spain*. London, 1930.

MADARIAGA, SALVADOR DE: *Anarquía o Jerarquía*. Madrid, 1935.

MENDIZÁBAL, ALFRED: *Aux Origines d'une Tragédie*. Paris, 1937. [Also in an English translation.]

MENÉNDEZ Y PELAYO, MARCELINO: *Historia de los Heterodoxos Españoles*, Vol. VII. (*Obras*, Vol. XIX, Madrid, 1932.)

MIGUÉLEZ, MANUEL F.: *Jansenismo y regalismo en España*, Valladolid, 1895.

MORENO, ENRIQUE: *Catholics and the Spanish State*. London, 1937. [A pamphlet written from the Popular Front standpoint.]

MOROTE, L.: *La Moral de la Derrota*. Madrid, 1900.

MOROTE, L.: *Los Frailes en España*. Madrid, 1904. [This and the last work are markedly anti-clerical.]

NOGUER, NARCISO: *La Acción Católica.* En la teoría y en la práctica, en España y en el extranjero. Madrid, *Razón y Fe*, 2 vols.

PARKER, A. A.: "The Catholic Church in Spain from 1800 till to-day," in *The Tablet*, March 5, 12, 19, 26, April 2, 1938. Also in revised form, as a pamphlet under the same title, London, Catholic Truth Society, 1938.

PARKER, A. A.: "The History and Policy of Carlism." In *Studies*, March, July, September 1937, Vol. XXVI, pp. 16–25, 207–22, 383–98.

PEERS, E. ALLISON: *Catalonia Infelix.* London, 1937. (This and the two following books have bibliographies.)

PEERS, E. ALLISON: *Our Debt to Spain.* London, 1938.

PEERS, E. ALLISON: *The Spanish Tragedy.* London, 1937 (6th edition, enlarged).

PEERS, E. ALLISON: *The Church in Spain, 1737–1937.* London, 1938.

PEIRÓ, P. FRANCISCO: *El Problema religioso-social de España.* Madrid, 1936.

PEMÁN, JOSÉ MARÍA: *¡Atención! ¡Atención!* Seville, 1937.

POLO Y PEYROLÓN, MANUEL: *El Anarquismo.* Valencia, 1894.

Preliminary Official Report on the Atrocities committed in Southern Spain in July and August 1936 by the Communist forces of the Madrid Government. London, 1936.

Report of a Group of Anglican and Free Churchmen who visited Spain, January 29 to February 9, 1937. London, 1937. [A pamphlet.]

RODRÍGUEZ SOLÍS, E.: *Historia del Partido Republicano.* Madrid, 1893.

Second and Third Official Reports on the Communist Atrocities committed in Southern Spain from July to October 1936, etc. London, 1937.

SEMPRÚN GURREA, JOSÉ MARÍA DE: *A Catholic looks at Spain.* London, 1937. [A Popular Front pamphlet.]

ZABALA Y LERA, P.: *Historia de España y de la Civilización Española*: Edad Contemporánea. Madrid, 1930, 2 vols. [A continuation of Altamira.]

INDEX

INDEX